The Northmen

The Emergence of Man

The Northmen

by Thomas Froncek
and the Editors
of TIME-LIFE Books

TIME-LIFE INTERNATIONAL
(Nederland) B.V.

The Author: THOMAS FRONCEK, a former staff member of LIFE and of American Heritage, is now a freelance writer and editor. He has long been interested in European and American cultural history and has written numerous articles about frontier and primitive peoples. Froncek's fascination with the Northmen stems from an earlier work, *The Barbarians and the Birth of Europe*, which, among other things, traced the paths of Scandinavian tribesmen who left the north and advanced eventually all the way to Rome.

The Consultant: BIRGITTA LINDEROTH WALLACE is a research assistant in the Section of Man at the Carnegie Museum of Natural History and Adjunct Research Associate Professor of the Department of Anthropology at the University of Pittsburgh. She has done most of her field work in her native Scandinavia but she has also participated for several years in the excavation of a Viking site at L'Anse aux Meadows, Newfoundland.

The Cover: Knee-deep in the strawlike grass of the windswept Scandinavian coast, two Bronze Age Danes raise graceful horns, called lurs, to their lips and blow a primeval fanfare of welcome to an incoming boat. The lur players and the boat were painted on a photograph of a beach in Jutland, Denmark, by Michael A. Hampshire.

Contents

Introduction

All too often people think that Scandinavian history begins with the Vikings, when in fact it stretches far back into the past—to a time when much of the north was still sheathed in glacial ice. At first only a few intrepid Stone Age hunters ventured into the new land being created by the ice's slow withdrawal—but as conditions changed, other groups followed. Eventually, a rich Scandinavian culture came into being —one shaped to a large extent by a demanding, often hostile environment.

Unique as their development was—in a harsh realm surrounded almost everywhere by water—the Northmen of prehistory were by no means cut off from other peoples. Although they seldom put their own stamp on their contemporaries, they were repeatedly at the receiving end of outside cultural impulses, ranging from influxes of eastern and western Europeans to lively trade dealings with other parts of Europe. Often what went on in the north was a microcosm of events occurring elsewhere—a circumstance of incalculable significance since the record of man's achievements here is, for fascinating reasons explained in this book, by and large more complete than it is in the rest of Europe.

In at least one important respect the contribution of Scandinavia to the comprehension of man's prehistory is measurable. As early as the 17th Century the Scandinavians formulated laws to prevent the destruction or removal of any ancient monument that had not been properly investigated and recorded. Encouraged by government interest, archaeological work soon became a popular pursuit. In fact, its popularity was such that one 18th Century writer, Ludvig Holberg, of Denmark, expressed amazement that work mean enough to constitute a suitable punishment for criminals was being performed willingly by hordes of happy volunteers.

To this day there are proportionately more working archaeologists in the Scandinavian countries than in any other part of the world, and the concern of ordinary laymen there with their own history and prehistory remains strong. Perhaps this preoccupation is natural in a population that has remained relatively homogeneous since the late Stone Age; many Scandinavians identify with the past—an attachment that has imbued archaeological relics with meaning that extends far beyond the fact of their physical survival.

My own involvement with the world of the Scandinavian past was nurtured by my father, who had a strong interest in history combined with a fondness for the out-of-doors and a curiosity about humanity at large. From my earliest childhood in Sweden I remember how every Sunday the entire family went off to the country, sauntering for endless hours through the woods, across meadows or along lake sides, where prehistoric remains everywhere dotted the landscape. Birds flew by, flowers grew at our feet, but the antiquities were the one and only thing that captured father's attention. He demonstrated to us children that they were not dead piles of stone or inane curiosities, but reverberant remembrances of people who were close to us, physically and spiritually. To me, to this day, the monuments and artifacts of the Northmen convey more eloquently than words the timelessness of human experience.

Birgitta Linderoth Wallace
Carnegie Museum of Natural History
Pittsburgh, Pennsylvania

Chapter One: An Awesome Past

It is the end of the Second Century B.C. The place: the northern borders of the Roman Republic in what is now Austria. On the edge of a deep forest that stretches—no man knows how far—beyond the Alps, a well-disciplined garrison of Roman legionnaires is suddenly attacked by a mob of howling, spear-waving warriors. Who they are, where they come from are as much a mystery as the forest from which they have emerged. Tall and sturdily built, with blond hair and fierce blue eyes, they wear animal totems on their helmets and strip themselves naked for battle, throwing themselves into the fray with the relish of men who love combat and have no fear of death. To the small, dark-haired Romans they look like demons.

Frightened and confused, the Romans fall back before the onslaught of this wild horde and are swept to defeat. The invaders push westwards into Gaul, plundering as they go, overwhelming one Roman division after another. In the spring of 102 B.C., they cross the Alps into Italy itself, shouting their war cries and sliding on their shields down the snowy slopes of the mountains into the Po Valley. Rome, in a panic, finally sends an army to crush them in 101 B.C. and carries off their chieftains in chains.

But the vanquished were yet to be the victors. This episode marked the first appearance in recorded history of a people—the Northmen—who would eventually overrun the Roman world and help shift the centre of European civilization from the Mediterranean to cooler lands beyond the Alps. They would also play a major rôle in shaping the laws, languages and customs of all Europe—and hence of America too. And from the startling remains of their culture, uniquely preserved in the soil and bogs of their northern homeland, would finally come, in the 20th Century, one of the most detailed pictures ever assembled of life in prehistoric Europe—from 10,000 B.C. to the beginning of the Christian era.

The homeland of these invaders lay along the shores of the Baltic and North seas in what is now Denmark, Norway and Sweden. In 500 B.C., when the weather pattern in the north turned unbearably cold and damp after a prolonged warm cycle, the Northmen began pouring south in search of a more hospitable domain. The first to terrorize the Roman world in the Second Century B.C. were Cimbrian and Teutonic tribesmen from Denmark's Jutland peninsula. In the centuries that followed, other Northmen swept across the continent in successive waves to pillage and conquer—and, incidentally, to leave behind evidence of their tribal identities in a host of European place names.

From Sweden—perhaps from the Swedish provinces of East and West Gotland—came the Goths, who first broke Roman power in the West. From the Danish island of Bornholm in the Baltic, once called Burgundarholm, may have come the Burgundians who founded the modern French province of Burgundy. From Vendsussel in the northern part of Denmark's Jutland peninsula may also have come the Vandals, who gave their name to the Spanish province of Andalusia—once Vandalusia. Lombards, from the region just below the Jutland peninsula,

Golden eyes ablaze, this two-and-a-half-inch Danish bronze figurine—possibly a fertility goddess—kneels to an unknown presence. Dating from the Bronze Age, the high point of Scandinavian prehistory, she wears a short cord skirt typical of her time and indicative of the warmer conditions then prevailing. A few hundred years later the cold of the Iron Age set in, driving hordes of Northmen south into Europe.

made northern Italy their home, and their fair-haired descendants may be seen there today strolling the streets of Verona and Milan. The Franks—whose kingdoms gave birth to France, Germany, Holland, Belgium and Switzerland—were originally a loose confederation of northern tribes that settled along the lower reaches of the Rhine. It is even possible that the first rulers of Russia were expatriate Swedes, descendants of a Scandinavian people who called themselves the Rus and who established trading settlements along the Volga and Dnieper as far back as 1800 B.C. No wonder the Sixth Century A.D. monk Jordanes, a Goth, proudly referred to Scandinavia in his *History of the Goths* as "the cradle of peoples" and "the womb of nations".

Yet, until fairly recently the ancestry of the Northmen remained largely a mystery. Nor did anyone realize that these "barbarians" had in fact enjoyed an advanced civilization of their own. Over the centuries the only real sources of information about them had been the writings of ancient Greeks and Romans. For a start, there was Pythias of Marseilles, a Greek, who about 350 B.C. made an extraordinary voyage to the tin mines of Britain and from there travelled across the sea to a place he called *ultima Thule* —probably Norway. Pythias described it as a cold, damp land where the summer sun never set and where the sea was choked with ice. The inhabitants, who kept few domestic animals, lived on grains, vegetables, wild fruits and roots, and in some regions they brewed a drink of honey and barley. Because the climate was so wet they had to thresh their grain in barns, for if threshed in the fields it would rot. Most of Pythias' tale was, inevitably, dismissed by the sensible folks back home as the preposterous yarn-

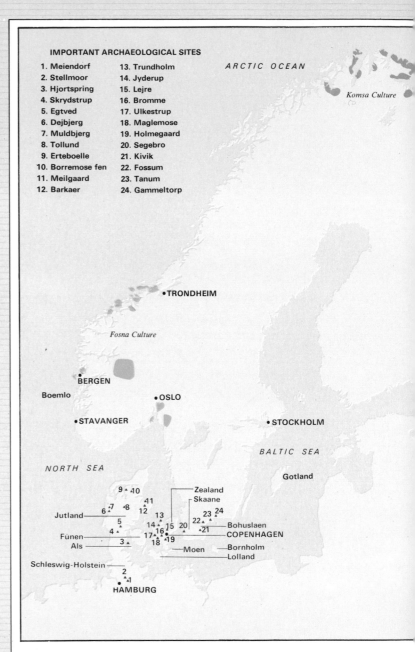

IMPORTANT ARCHAEOLOGICAL SITES

1. Meiendorf
2. Stellmoor
3. Hjortspring
4. Skrydstrup
5. Egtved
6. Dejbjerg
7. Muldbjerg
8. Tollund
9. Erteboelle
10. Borremose fen
11. Meilgaard
12. Barkaer
13. Trundholm
14. Jyderup
15. Lejre
16. Bromme
17. Ulkestrup
18. Maglemose
19. Holmegaard
20. Segebro
21. Kivik
22. Fossum
23. Tanum
24. Gammeltorp

Realm of the Northmen
Important archaeological sites discussed in this volume are keyed to the numbered triangles on the map of Scandinavia above; modern localities are identified by name. The sites range from a 14,000 B.C. camp of reindeer hunters at Meiendorf (1) to a First Century B.C. Iron Age community (6). The two major early reindeer-hunting cultures are indicated by colour: orange for the Komsa complex in the north and green for the Fosna settlements in the southwest. The sites are most heavily concentrated on the Danish peninsula of Jutland and near-by islands for two reasons: the first settlers arrived from the south and advanced only as glaciers retreated north, and the Danes have been particularly diligent in the pursuit of prehistory.

A Scandinavian Chronology

Some highlights in the prehistory and archaeology of the Northmen and the approximate dates:

240,000 B.C.
Earliest traces of human presence in Scandinavia.

14,000 B.C.
First-known sacrifices of prey in sacred bodies of water.

12,000-9000 B.C.
First evidence of reindeer hunters' campsites in Denmark and southern Sweden.

8000-4000 B.C.
Maglemose hunter culture in Denmark.

8000-2000 B.C.
Fosna and Komsa hunter cultures in Norway and Sweden.

6000 B.C.
Earliest evidence that boats were used in Scandinavia.

5000 B.C.
Early kitchen-midden culture in Denmark.

4300 B.C.
Earliest Scandinavian pottery.

4200-3800 B.C.
Domesticated animals brought to Scandinavia from the south. Building of stone grave monuments begins.

3300 B.C.
First passage graves in Denmark and southern Sweden.

2800 B.C.
Influx of nomadic immigrants from eastern Europe.

1800 B.C.
Beginning of Scandinavian Bronze Age.

1500 B.C.
Ritual sacrifices continue, but jewellery, weapons and other valuables are also tossed into sacred waters.

500 B.C.
Beginning of Iron Age in Scandinavia. Sacrifices expanded to include captured booty and human beings.

350 B.C.
First mention of Northmen by a Greek writer.

A.D. 98
Tacitus describes customs and manners of northern tribes.

spinning of a sailor who had been at sea too long.

Next there was Julius Caesar's description of the Northmen as he encountered them on his campaigns in Gaul in 60 B.C.: "They spend all their lives in hunting and military pursuits," he wrote, "and believe that continence makes a man grow taller and stronger." Nevertheless, he reported, they were not prudes, for "men and women bathe together in the rivers and wear nothing except skins and short cloaks of reindeer hide, which leave most of the body bare". He observed that their diet was composed almost exclusively of meat, cheese and milk and that "they do not go in much for agriculture".

A little more than a century later, the Roman historian Tacitus had a good deal to add about the customs and character of the Northmen in a book called *The Germania*. He described their sacred groves and the forms of worship that went on in them; he was also amazed by their "drinking bouts lasting all day and all night" and by their constant feasting that was also "an occasion for discussing such affairs as the ending of feuds and the arrangement of marriage alliances". Some of the northern clans, Tacitus reported, preferred to fight at night, and cleverly blacked their shields and dyed their bodies, thus inspiring "mortal panic" in their enemies. Other northern tribes were powerful on the sea as well as on the land and possessed ships "with a prow at each end, so that they are always facing the right way to put into shore".

All this made fascinating reading, but how much of it was true? Tacitus claimed, for instance, that the most northerly of the Scandinavians lived along a sea, sluggish and almost stagnant, that was "believed to be the boundary that girdles the earth, because the

As snows melt in the weak warmth of a Scandinavian spring,
the terrain beneath is laid bare—suggesting how the land
looked 18,000 years ago when the glacier began its retreat and
made possible human settlement of northern Europe.

last radiance of the setting sun lingers on here until dawn". Undoubtedly this was so, said Tacitus, for "so far, and no further does the world extend". And Caesar, in describing the land of the people he called *Germani*, told of hearing about a fascinating kind of elk that lived there. These beasts looked like large goats, he reported, but "their legs have no joints . . . and they never lie down to rest; if they fall down by accident they are unable to get up again". They slept standing up, leaning against trees, Caesar averred; hunters captured them by sawing partway through tree trunks so that the trees collapsed when the animals leaned against them. That Caesar could accept such a yarn attests to how little the Romans really knew about Europe's northern lands and people.

The perspective of the Greek and Roman writers was often distorted, too, by a common human failing: their myopic view of themselves as enlightened and civilized and of the intruding Northmen as naked brutes huddling miserably over their campfires in woodland clearings. As the eminent English archaeologist Geoffrey Bibby has pointedly observed: "It was the Greeks who, in their arrogance, applied the term *barbarian* to peoples enjoying a civilization different from their own; and the Romans, inheriting the idea, assumed always that their fluctuating frontier was the dividing-line between urbane civilization and uncouth savagery."

Yet, until a little more than 100 years ago, the ancient Greek and Roman writers remained a chief source of information about the Northmen. All through the Middle Ages and in fact right up to the middle of the 19th Century, man's existence was generally thought to have begun with Adam and Eve, whose descendants multiplied and wandered to the far corners of the earth. In this dispersal Europe was assumed to have been populated relatively recently. Thus, the great stone monuments and burial mounds that dotted the landscape of northern Europe from Britain to Sweden, and the stone and pottery artifacts that were constantly being turned up by the ploughs of farmers in Scandinavia and elsewhere were lumped together as belonging to a vague age described simply as Gothic or pre-Roman.

The notion that the prehistoric peoples of northern Europe, to say nothing of the rest of the continent, could, over thousands of years, have evolved distinctive cultures of their own dates back only to the 19th Century and to the birth in Scandinavia of the modern science of archaeology. Since then, all sorts of amazing finds have proved, without a doubt, that the Northmen's ancestry is much more ancient, and their culture much more varied and sophisticated than anyone had imagined. Moreover, these finds show that the saga of the Northmen unfolded against a violent natural backdrop—of retreating glaciers and rising land masses, of changing patterns of vegetation and radical shifts in weather.

The first people for whom the archaeological record speaks quite clearly were nomadic reindeer hunters who arrived in Scandinavia some 12,000 years ago. Setting up camp perhaps only a few days' walk from the wall of glacial ice that still covered much of northern Europe, they hunted and fished on the tundra with spears and harpoons of stone and bone. But more remarkably, they were also equipped with the bow and arrow—a new, efficient weapon; the first confirmation of this invention's use in Europe comes from their campsites. Some 5,000 or 6,000 years later, when the ice had receded, the descendants of these people

Farmer and part-time archaeologist Ragnar Pedersen, with his wife, examines a piece of pottery that he dug from his land in Denmark's northern Jutland. One of the few private citizens permitted by the National Museum to undertake excavations, Pedersen has unearthed some 3,000 objects from the Stone, Bronze and Iron ages within a five-mile radius of his farmhouse.

were still leading a nomadic existence, but they had learned to cope with forest conditions as well as tundra. They chopped down trees with hafted, or handled, stone axes that are among the earliest such tools found anywhere in the world. And they used the trees to fashion dugout canoes and perhaps the framework for skin boats, which took them through ice-filled northern waters.

Around 4200 B.C. the idea of farming and of permanent dwellings was introduced into Scandinavia. Gradually the conditions of life improved, and around 2000 B.C. there began a period that can be called prehistoric Scandinavia's golden age. Blessed by a change in climate that made the Northlands as warm as southern France is today, the Northmen prospered. Their merchant mariners traded in amber and furs; Scandinavian metalsmiths shaped imported bronze into splendid weapons and ornaments; Scandinavian princes were rich enough to be buried amid magnificent gold and bronze trappings.

Much of this new picture of the Northmen's ancient past began to emerge with the work of a handful of dedicated 19th Century Scandinavian scholars who laid the foundations for the modern science of archaeology. The first of them, Rasmus Nyerup, was a professor at the University of Copenhagen, whose hobby was searching Denmark's bogs and burial mounds for antiquities. Nyerup set up a small museum in the university to display his finds, but he felt that they should be collated and studied with other artifacts like them in order to determine their relative ages. "Everything that has come down to us from heathendom is wrapped in a thick fog," he observed. "It belongs to a space of time which we cannot measure. We know that it is older than

Christendom, but whether by a couple of years or a couple of centuries, or even by more than a millennium, we can do no more than guess."

As a result of Nyerup's lobbying, the Danish government in 1819 created the Royal Museum of Nordic Antiquities, now called the National Museum, and appointed a young man named Christian Jurgensen Thomsen to be its curator. Thomsen was the son of a merchant and shipowner and was employed in his father's business at the time. But like Nyerup he was enormously keen on Danish antiquities and thus ready to devote his energies to the new job. Charged in his duties with bringing order to the museum's chaotic collection, and with no system to guide him, Thomsen drew upon his experience as a clerk in his father's warehouses. First he divided the artifacts by category—stone, metal, ceramic. Then he divided them by their apparent functions—tools, weapons, religious relics, household utensils.

Gradually, as he studied and compared the different groups, Thomsen concluded that the objects of stone had been made earlier than those of metal and that the bronze artifacts seemed to precede those of iron. He was thus the first to divide prehistory into three major chronological periods, and his designations are still in use today—Stone Age, Bronze Age, Iron Age. He was also the first to demonstrate that prehistoric man, too, had evolved culturally. As a result of his efforts, Thomsen would eventually be known as "the father of European prehistory".

If the existence of Thomsen's Three Ages now seems too obvious ever to have been questioned—or even to have needed discovery—his theory was long the subject of debate among his contemporaries. Published in 1836 under the title *Guide to Scandina-*

As curator of Denmark's Royal Museum of Nordic Antiquities, Christian J. Thomsen, "the father of European prehistory," periodically took time out from his duties to lecture visitors personally on the exhibits. To bring history vividly alive, he had a favourite trick, recorded in this 1846 drawing: he used to take a heavy, gold neck-ring—worn thousands of years before by an unknown ancestor—and place it around a child's neck.

vian Antiquities—and soon translated into German, French and English—his thesis was widely studied and much discussed. Many European antiquarians, particularly the Germans, insisted that even if the Three Ages did apply to Denmark's prehistory, there was no reason to suppose that the system could be applied to the rest of Europe. Many Danish authorities, meanwhile, argued that whether people used stone tools or metal ones could have been as much a matter of economics as of chronology, and, indeed, it has since been established that in some localities poorer folk continued to use stone tools long after richer neighbours had switched to metal ones. But none of this invalidated Thomsen's theory, which little by little won acceptance among students of prehistory.

That the Three Ages eventually came to be accepted was due in large part to the efforts of one of Thomsen's pupils, a brilliant and energetic young man by the name of Jens Jacob Asmussen Worsaae, who has since been accorded recognition as the world's first professional archaeologist. Born in Jutland in 1821, the son of a sheriff, Worsaae was a country boy whose interest in antiquity was aroused early by the great burial mounds that dotted the landscape near his home and by the flint arrowheads and stone axes that ploughmen kept turning up almost in his backyard. He was already an enthusiastic collector of antiquities by the age of fifteen, when his father sent him to Copenhagen to prepare for a law career. On his arrival in the capital, Worsaae headed straight for the National Museum and presented himself to Christian Thomsen. Soon he was spending all his spare time at the museum or out in the field, where he began digging into the grave mounds that even today can be found just outside of Copenhagen. It

was not enough, he observed, to study objects in museums; one must examine and carefully compare the places in which the antiquities are usually found.

Applying Thomsen's Three Age system to his own fieldwork, Worsaae analysed grave sites to determine whether they belonged to the Stone Age, the Bronze Age or the Iron Age. Each age, it soon became apparent, had its own distinctive burial forms and customs. In time Worsaae even refined Thomsen's Three Age system. He noticed, for instance, tremendous differences in the style and technique of stone tools: some were crudely chipped; others were beautifully ground and polished. To account for these differences, he divided the Stone Age into an early and a late period, calling the former the Old Stone Age and the latter the New.

As a result of his innovative approach Worsaae attracted the patronage of, first, King Christian VIII of Denmark and then of Christian's successor, Frederick VII. Both monarchs were avid antiquarians, a trait that seems to run in Scandinavia's royal families. The late King Gustav of Sweden was a respected amateur archaeologist, and his granddaughter, the queen of Denmark, followed in his footsteps. This royal Scandinavian fascination with the past extends far back in time. In 1630, long before anyone dreamed of studying prehistory in a systematic way, Gustavus Adolphus III of Sweden appointed two scholars to travel through the countryside compiling a catalogue of rune stones—ancient slabs engraved with an early form of writing—and similar objects.

Thanks to the interest in his profession taken by the royal house, Worsaae was appointed antiquarian to the king, and in this capacity accompanied Frederick on annual archaeological digs—splendid expeditions that progressed by royal carriage, complete with footmen and champagne lunches, and that enjoyed the muscle power of soldiers detailed to do the actual digging of the sites.

The work of Nyerup, Thomsen and Worsaae forced a dramatic change in man's thinking about his past. No longer was it possible to consider European prehistory as a relatively brief span of time between the Garden of Eden and the building of the pyramids during which little had happened, little had changed. No longer was it possible to believe that man's roots lay only in the Mediterranean world. Together, Nyerup, Thomsen and Worsaae helped to awaken Europe to its prehistoric past and gave students of antiquity a structure and a method for penetrating that past. The Three Age system, although it has since been greatly refined, was the starting point for the orderly and systematic exploration of prehistory. The science of archaeology has come a long way since then. Indeed, in Scandinavia itself the history of man reaches back much further than Nyerup, Thomsen and Worsaae ever dreamed it could.

It now appears that man may have been there as early as 240,000 years ago and certainly at least 80,000 years ago—though the evidence in either case is hardly profuse. In support of the much earlier date, the evidence consists entirely of several roughly chipped pieces of flint found in Denmark a few years ago; they have been dated geologically by taking into account the surroundings in which they lay, and are still being studied. Supporting the later date is a handful of bones that were split open in order to extract the marrow—a sure sign of man's handiwork. The bones belong to a species of fallow deer that flourished in northern Europe around 100,000 B.C. and

became extinct about 75,000 B.C. when the glaciers advanced down from the north, blanketing much of the European continent in ice.

Who worked the flints? This is a tantalizing question and one that may never be answered adequately. The only skeletal materials old enough to provide a basis for speculation are two skulls found in northern Europe: Swanscombe man from England, dated at 250,000 years, and Steinheim man, from Germany, dated at 200,000 years. Both are considered to be pre-Neanderthal types.

The cracked bones of the fallow deer, on the other hand, may well be the remains of a Neanderthal's meal. Neanderthals were roaming Europe at the time, and they are believed to have ventured as far north as Scandinavia in pursuit of game. The chances of finding further evidence of their stay there, however, are slim. The bulldozer action of the mile-thick ice sheet swept away all traces of their campsites and scattered their relics.

For thousands of years the same ice sheet that obliterated the tracks of the Neanderthals also shaped the contours of the Scandinavian landscape, providing it with many of its present-day features. Advancing and retreating with fluctuations in the climate, the ice ground down rocks and boulders and dragged the abrasive debris over the earth, levelling hills, carving mountains, cutting gorges, scouring out or filling in valleys. At times the ice pack was so thick that the land literally sagged under its weight. There was one period when all Norway, Sweden, what is now the Baltic Sea and much of northern and eastern Denmark were depressed by the massive glacier into one enormous saucer.

Reality and myth were combined to humorous effect in this 1861 Danish sketch. The scene commemorates the removal of a Bronze Age oak coffin from its grave as Jens Worsaae, the world's first professional archaeologist, directs the workmen (pointing figure, centre). Commenting on the activity from the mouth of a cave (at right) is a tiny troll, the legendary inhabitant of the Scandinavian countryside.

When the ice sheet began its final retreat, some 18,000 years ago, the weight on the land gradually lightened and the land itself began to rise; northern Sweden is now almost a thousand feet higher than it was when the last ice age ended, and some former shorelines stand high above the water. According to geologists, northeastern Sweden is still rising at the rate of three feet every 100 years.

All these great changes had tremendous consequences for Scandinavia. The melting ice caused sea levels to rise, and seas appeared where there had been none. The seas, in turn, redrew the coastlines. The melting ice also pockmarked the inland terrain with hundreds of shallow, ice-cold lakes—lakes that through two quite different natural processes subsequently yielded two important kinds of archaeological data. One is a pattern of sedimentation that accurately charts the chronology of the withdrawing glaciers and the Northmen's advance into the emerging new land. The other is the peat that built up in the lakes and has marvellously preserved, through chemical action, some of the otherwise perishable organic materials immersed in it centuries ago.

The sediment consisted of the annual fallout of the melting glaciers—the ground-up bits of rock swept up by the ice. These particles of rock were carried into the lakes where the runoff collected and settled to the bottom in a predictable sequence: heavy materials first, followed by layers of increasingly lighter materials. The final layer of extremely fine clay continued to filter down for many months, sometimes well into the following winter, when the surface of the lake had long since refrozen. Because the lakes were relatively undisturbed by currents and tides, the thickness of each year's sedimentary layers—which

Challenging Lands Born of Water and Ice

By 500 B.C., the beginning of the Iron Age, Scandinavia's terrain bore little resemblance to the places inhabited by the earliest Northmen some 10,000 years earlier. Land that had been dry was now drowned in sea water. What had been a huge, fresh-water lake strewn with icebergs was a salty sea —the Baltic. And land that had been buried under a giant ice sheet was open and habitable.

The glacier that once covered much of the Northern Hemisphere was responsible for these changes. As the deep ice melted and shrank, it exposed increasingly more land and, at the same time, it dumped immense quantities of meltwater into the lakes and seas, causing their levels to rise. Moreover, the land that had been depressed by the enormous weight of the glacier sprang upwards; where the ice had been as much as two miles deep, the glacier had exerted some six million pounds of pressure upon every square yard of earth and rock. Relieved of this huge burden, the Scandinavian peninsula rebounded, sometimes at the fantastic rate of three feet in just 10 years.

During the tenure of the Northmen, the race between the rising water and

12,000 - 8300 B.C.	8300 - 7000 B.C.

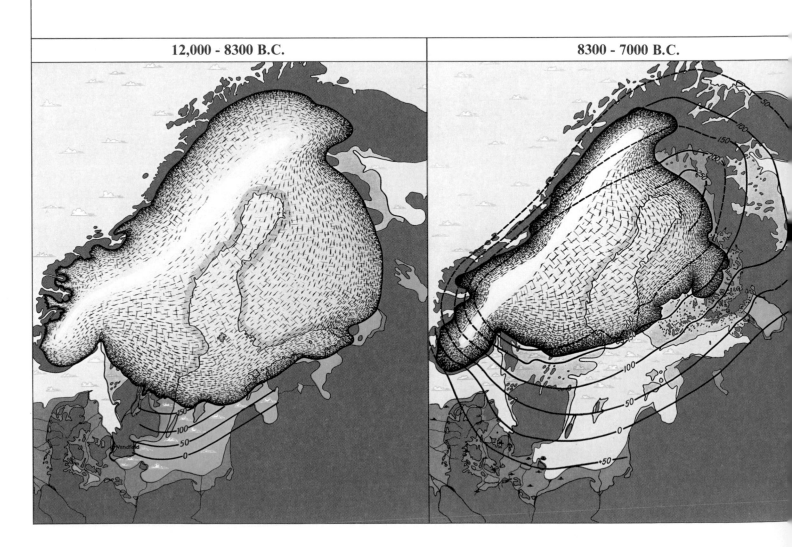

the rising land caused the dramatic changes charted on the maps below. (Contour lines, measured in metres, cover only those areas where there is sufficient information to permit sound approximations of the elevations of both land and ice.)

In the period from 12,000 to 8300 B.C., the Baltic was a relatively small body, bounded on the south by land and on the north by ice (*first map*); because it had no access to open ocean —and because its sources were fresh inland water—it was, in fact, a lake. Later, from 8300 to 7000 B.C. (*second map*), the glacier that had formed the

Baltic's western barrier retreated and exposed a dip in the land, which allowed the north Atlantic's salt water to flow into the Baltic. By 7000 to 5000 B.C. (*third map*) the glacier had dwindled sharply to only two small patches. Unburdened, the land rose still more—and again landlocked the Baltic; this time it was a far bigger lake, with shorelines approximating those of today. But the Baltic was due to become a sea again; by 5000 to 500 B.C. (*fourth map*) the land bridge across southern Sweden was flooded and once again the fresh and salt waters of the two bodies intermingled.

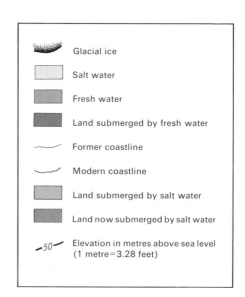

	Glacial ice
	Salt water
	Fresh water
	Land submerged by fresh water
	Former coastline
	Modern coastline
	Land submerged by salt water
	Land now submerged by salt water
—50—	Elevation in metres above sea level (1 metre = 3.28 feet)

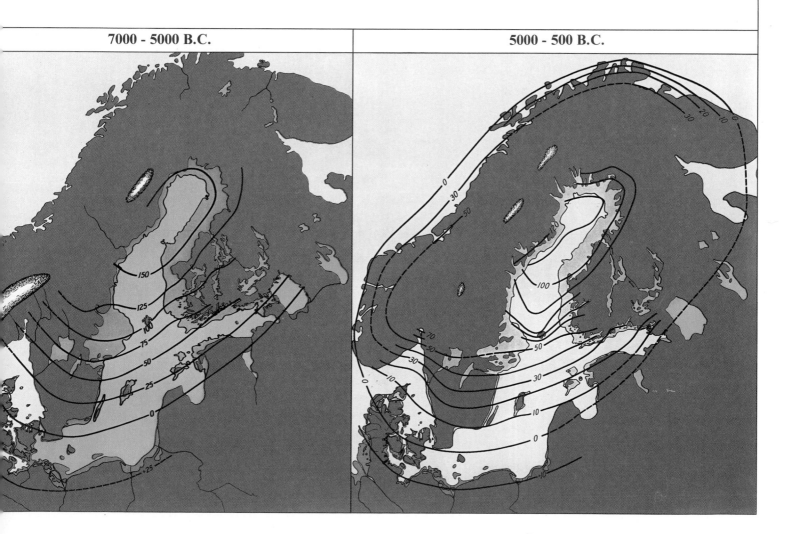

7000 - 5000 B.C.

5000 - 500 B.C.

scientists call varves—can be read like case histories of glacial action, revealing when the ice melted quickly and when it barely melted at all. In 1910, a Swedish geologist, Baron Gerard de Geer, used this consistent pattern of sedimentation to establish the first system for dating the glaciers' withdrawal.

While the sediment was sifting down, the glacial lakes were also becoming receptacles for another sort of material. Lichens, mosses and sedges growing along the shore were gradually clogging the lakes. As this thick vegetation died, the chill waters prevented its rapid deterioration by bacteria. The water reacted with the chemicals in the plants to embalm them in the form of peat. By a similar chemical action the peat bogs, in turn, embalmed anything interred in them. Thus, all sorts of things tossed into the bogs by man—axe handles, clothing, animals, even human beings—have been preserved almost intact. Indeed, so efficient was the process that scientists examining the body of one Iron Age man found in a bog discovered what he had eaten before dying.

To come upon someone who has been dead 2,400 years, whose every hair is in place and whose fingerprints are still as clear as on the day he died, is, to say the least, an astonishing experience. In the past, the astonishment was frequently tinged with alarm. When the first "bog man" was accidentally exhumed in Denmark on a June day in 1450, the local priest urged his discoverers to put him back in the bog and leave him to the elves who had lured him there. No one at the time could have conceived of the corpse's great antiquity, much less its archaeological value.

At least 166 "bog people" have since been uncovered in Denmark alone. But they are only one category among the many incredible finds in Scandinavia that have thrown startling light on the emergence of man in prehistoric Europe. So numerous are these finds and so often have they turned up in unexpected places that it is no wonder Christian Thomsen made a special point of personally guiding Danish peasants through his new museum. He realized that if they appreciated the objects they turned up during routine tilling, he would have a large army of researchers working without fee: "It is by them," he wrote, "that we shall have our collections enlarged." And no wonder, too, that Scandinavians, surrounded as they are by the highly visible evidence of their ancient past, have been so keenly interested in lifting what Rasmus Nyerup called "the thick fog that has come down to us from heathendom".

Denmark's Lejre— Building a Window into Prehistory

Built to be burned, a thatched house goes up in flames. At right, scientific instruments record the progress of the conflagration.

Passionate explorers of the past, modern Scandinavians have developed extraordinary new ways of finding out how people lived in northern Europe in prehistoric times. At a site near the town of Lejre, 25 miles west of Copenhagen, Danish scientists have been testing their theories about the past in a series of fascinating experiments involving plants, animals and people.

Basing their work on solid archaeological evidence, they have set about constructing duplicates of Iron Age houses, tilling fields with copies of ancient ploughs, weaving cloth on reconstructions of prehistoric looms and turning it into clothing. In the process they have discovered—among other things—exactly how the houses were built, how the tools were used and how many acres of grain it took to feed a family of six or eight. In the experiment above, they even set one of the reconstructions on fire to see how closely its ruins would match the charred remains of actual Iron Age dwellings that have been uncovered.

The Village Where Past is Present

A living experiment in prehistory, the research centre at Lejre was founded in 1964, and today spreads over 50 acres of Danish fields and woodlands. Its focus is a re-created village (*right*) of the early Iron Age—the period from about 500 B.C. to A.D. 400.

No mere tourist attraction, the settlement is a working laboratory. Here, aided by student volunteers who live and sometimes dress like prehistoric farmers, the Lejre scientists measure everything from the body heat given off by animals stabled indoors to the length of time it takes for a thatched wattle-and-daub house to disintegrate after it has been abandoned.

Nestled between marsh and hill, the houses at Lejre, like their Iron Age counterparts, lie along an east-west axis, with hearth and living quarters at the western end of each and pens for livestock at the eastern end. An encircling branch fence keeps grazing animals from nibbling at the thatch.

Wearing copies of clothes found in Iron Age graves and in bogs, a family of volunteers will see how well animal-skin capes, tunics and shoes withstand dampness and cold. Woollen leggings offer protection against burrs and nettles as well as against the Danish chill.

A horsehide, with the bones of the skull and legs left intact, hangs from a pole outside the village compound (at far right, above; and close up, right). The practice revives a prehistoric Danish rite in which the horse may have symbolized strength and power.

Rediscovering Prehistoric Fare

Scrupulously scientific in duplicating the living conditions of Iron Age Danes, the researchers at Lejre have also explored in detail the ancient methods of food production.

The efficiency of the prehistoric plough—the ard—has been tested in various kinds of soil, using draught animals that closely approximate in size and appearance breeds believed to have been used at the time.

In the fields thus turned up, scientists have planted the kinds of crops that, according to pollen analysis and seed remains, were sown by Iron Age farmers: flax, barley and emmer and einkorn wheat. In the autumn, the harvesting has been done with copies of ancient sickles.

Finally, volunteers living one winter in the draughty houses undertook the chore of crushing the grain into flour, kneading it into bread and making it into porridge (*right*). As much as three hours were required, they found, to grind a day's worth of coarse meal.

Preparing the day's food, a young woman kneels at a stone gristmill and grinds grain into flour. Beneath the runner and the rester, as the millstones are called, a sheepskin helps to keep the dirt on the hard-packed clay floor from becoming mixed with the grain. Overhead, cuts of meat, suspended from rafters to dry and cure, dangle in the warm smoke of the hearth fire.

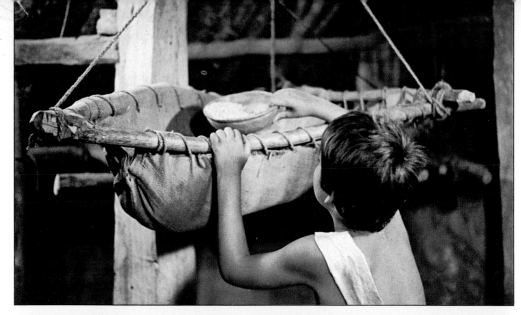

Using a replica of an ancient Danish bowl, a young Lejre volunteer scoops grain from a cloth-covered drying rack. Hung from the rafters in the lofts of experimental thatched houses, such racks serve to keep the grain out of reach of vermin. The smoke from the hearth, drifting through the loft, gives added protection against rodents.

Copies of an Iron Age bowl, knife and wooden trough are used by this girl to turn the gritty flour into bread dough. Loaves of "fireplace" bread baked in the ashes of the hearth fire have been discovered at Iron Age settlements. There was little or no furniture in Iron Age houses, so grinding, baking and most other work at Lejre have to be done while sitting or kneeling on the clay floor.

Bringing to Life Forgotten Skills

Reviving lost arts, researchers at Lejre have painstakingly re-created ancient crafts and have passed their discoveries on to present-day artisans.

By studying the style and the chemical structure of ancient pieces of pottery and by experimenting with different techniques of firing, potters have been able to produce accurate copies of the Iron Age originals.

Similarly, drawing upon information as diverse as loom weights dug up at archaeological sites and paintings on Greek vases, weavers at Lejre have reconstructed the upright loom of prehistoric times and have used it to reproduce the woollen costumes of the Iron Age.

This pottery kiln, a type used in northern Europe 2,500 years ago, is constructed of clay that has been packed around a frame of twigs and hardened by fire. The intense heat carried up by draughts from the wood-filled firebox, at the bottom of the kiln, hardens the raw pottery stacked inside the bulbous oven (top).

Seen through the kiln's draught hole, bowls glow in the light of the fire. Nested within some bowls are clay andirons. After the firing, they were used to secure cooking pots over an open hearth. The holes in the andirons made it possible to lift them out of the fire with sticks.

The hand-spun yarn being woven here, although coarse and thick, provided valuable insight into the ancient techniques of spinning. Similarly, the upright warp-weighted loom—which disappeared in the Middle Ages after centuries of use in the Northlands—is now being used to teach weaving to thousands of Danish school children.

Wearing a robe of homespun identical to ancient garments, a research assistant weaves cloth on a standing loom. Replicas of ancient fabrics are the product of years of research, involving microscopic study of Iron Age textiles and the breeding of special sheep to produce the proper kind of wool. Long hours are spent spinning thread to the right coarseness and strength and adjusting the loom so that the length and number of threads correspond to those in the original cloth.

Living Quarters for Man and Beast

Experiments with animals have yielded bonuses for both man and beast at Lejre. During part of one winter, the researchers shared the living quarters with livestock. That such an arrangement was common practice in prehistoric times is evident from horse and cattle bones found in charred house ruins. As the researchers learned, the animals' body heat helped to make the chilly house liveable. Some of the animals so used were products of careful breeding experiments aimed at approximating now-extinct breeds. When turned loose in the spring, the animals were watched to see what impact they would have on the vegetation of near-by pastures and forests.

A hairy pig—hardy, quick and well adapted to living in the forest as its ancestors were—was produced by breeding farm pigs with wild boars.

Using a long branch as a pitchfork, a research assistant cleans up the stable area—a few feet from where the family works, eats and sleeps.

Threshing is done indoors in the passageway between the living quarters and stable, where persistent draughts help blow away the chaff.

The loft over the cattle pens, used to store fodder and grain, makes a good place for this boy to sleep—provided the smoke does not get too thick.

A Warm Focus for the Home

Throughout the long, dark months of the Scandinavian Iron Age winter, the hearth fire was the centre of activity. Huddled close to its meagre warmth, women worked at their weaving, did the cooking and ground the grain, while the men prepared their farm tools for spring use, or their weapons for an occasional morning's hunt.

Skins of oxen and horses suspended over the fire helped keep flying sparks from reaching the dry roof thatch. There was no chimney hole, which would have permitted rain and snow to enter; instead air holes were placed under the apex of the roof at either end of the house. The cross draught carried the hearth smoke from one end of the dwelling, through the loft and out the other opening. At the same time, the warmth of the livestock was drawn into the living area.

Dressed in woollens, their feet swathed in animal hides, Lejre researchers share a meal beside an open-hearth fire. The grist stones, the storage jar, the clay andiron (foreground) and the meat smoking over the fire—all these would be familiar to Northmen of the Iron Age. But whether they had beds, like the one shown here, or slept on the floor close to the hearth, wrapped in sheepskins and cattle hides, has yet to be determined.

"Beneath the arms of the giant of ice grew man-child and maid together" runs the Old Norse myth of man's beginnings as set down in the epic *Poetic Edda*. And in a sense the myth is right. As fast as the glaciers of the last ice age retreated in a northeasterly direction, men followed after—to live in the glaciers' shadow. By 10,000 B.C., when the edge of the ice skirted the coastline of the Scandinavian peninsula, men were living across the water in Denmark (*pages 20-21*). As the ice sheet continued to withdraw, nomads moved into the newly green meadows of moss, lichens and sedges that fringed the shores of southern Sweden and western Norway. By 8000 B.C., while most of the Scandinavian peninsula's interior still lay sheathed in ice, hunters were establishing footholds on the Norwegian headlands that border the Arctic Ocean and on the islands as well—braving an environment few humans had hazarded before.

All these earliest Northmen were hunters, and undoubtedly they were descendants of the Cro-Magnon reindeer hunters who roamed Europe beginning perhaps 35,000 years ago. The northern hunters pursued the ancient way of life, but also over the course of many thousands of years they gradually responded to the challenges of their environment by adopting various innovations, ranging from bows and arrows to skis and sledges.

The story of one such northward trek begins around 14,000 B.C. in a wide valley in the southern

part of Jutland in what is now the German province of Schleswig-Holstein. The late spring landscape is a patchwork of tiny tundra flowers and the air is filled with the sound of meltwater trickling off the near-by hillsides. Though pockets of snow still lie on the higher ground and the temperature some days hovers just above freezing, a few geese have already begun to build their nests along the shores of the valley's frigid lakes. Foxes, lemmings, badgers and ptarmigans —arctic grouse—scurry for cover in thickets of birch and spruce and larch. In the meadows herds of reindeer have settled down to graze and calve, ending their long migration from their winter pastures hundreds of miles to the south.

Near one of the lakes a small band of reindeer hunters—numbering no more than 20—has begun to set up camp. Bearing their tents and household gear on their backs, they have been following the reindeer for weeks, ever since the first scent of spring set the herds drifting northwards in search of new pastures. Now that the herds have reached the northern limits of their migration, the band of hunters can look forward to at least four months of settled life. Carefully selecting a spot that offers plenty of water as well as some protection from the chill winds that blow across the tundra even in summer, they pitch their tents of reindeer hide on the shores of a lake.

Life for these hunters is closely intertwined with that of the reindeer. Its flesh feeds them. Its hide, made into tents and clothing, keeps them warm. Its sinews give them thread for sewing and for attaching flint points to their spears. Its teeth provide them with ornaments and its bones and antlers are among their prime tool materials. So intimate is the bond between hunter and prey that the reindeer spirit is a

Valued possessions, these 10,000-year-old amber amulets —each about two inches long—were carried by Scandinavian nomads, apparently to bring them luck on hunts. Some are carved into animal shapes, like the bear (top), the swimming fowl (bottom left) and the moose-like elk's head (centre), and nearly all are decorated with incised designs of dots and lines.

force to be propitiated, lest it withdraw its bounty. Hence, the hunters carry with them amulets: one of these, a small amber disc, bears the scratched outlines of reindeers' legs and antlers. Used with the proper ceremony, the little charm is believed to encourage good hunting.

Meanwhile, as a mark of respect for the reindeer spirit, the newly encamped hunters sacrifice the choicest animal from their first day's kill, a two-year-old doe. Weighting the carcass with a 20-pound stone enclosed in its rib cage, they throw the doe as far out into the lake as they can. In so doing they are resorting to a form of sacrifice that will persist among the Northmen right up to historical times: the practice of making offerings to gods by placing gifts in bodies of water.

All through the summer the hunters live beside the lake—eating, sleeping, hunting, shaping and refining their flint tools and spear points, fashioning new clothing of reindeer hide. In the autumn, when the reindeer herd heads south, the hunters trail along too. But they leave behind at the lakeside camp objects of various kinds: the bones of their kills, an array of well-used flint tools, antler axes and spear points, and the skeleton of the sacrificial doe. Together these will be enough to give men of another age an extraordinarily clear picture of what the reindeer hunters' life was like.

The camp just described lies in a grassy meadow now called Meiendorf, near the town of Ahrensburg. It was excavated in 1932 by a man named Alfred Rust. Born in 1900 in Hamburg and trained as an electrician, Rust became an enthusiastic student of prehistory. In 1930 he chucked his job and set off by bicycle for Syria, 2,800 miles away, expressly to find and explore an Upper Palaeolithic settlement. In 1931 he repeated the trip, again by bicycle. But Rust was also fascinated by the prehistoric peoples of his own area, and he knew that ancient artifacts regularly turned up in the valley where Ahrensburg lay, just 10 miles outside Hamburg.

The clue that eventually led him to the reindeer hunters' camp was a curious type of oblong flint implement, shaped like a parrot's beak, that occurred in special abundance on one particular slope of the valley, just above a watery peat bog. Rust called the unusual implement a *Papageienschnabelklingen-endhohlkratzerbohrerschraber*: a conglomerate word that means parrot-beak-blade-end-concave-scratcher-borer-scraper; eventually, and more reasonably, Rust referred to the object simply as a *Zinke*, or point.

The *Zinke* was cruder and heavier than later Stone Age implements that had been retrieved in northern Europe. Unfortunately, years of ploughing had so churned up the slope that archaeologists could no longer hope to identify the *Zinke* with a single culture. But Rust had a hunch that in the bog at the foot of the slope he might find an undisturbed site that would tell him something about the men who had made and used the *Zinke*.

Like similar peat bogs all over northern Europe, this one had once been a glacial lake that was gradually overrun by vegetation. Rust guessed that if people had lived along the lake millennia ago, they probably would have tossed their refuse into the water—even as people do today. And very likely it was still there, buried beneath the accumulation of peat.

In July 1933, armed with a hand pump and aided by six volunteers, Rust began digging along the shoreline of the former lake. On the original lake bottom, beneath seven feet of peat, he came upon a reindeer antler from which an 18-inch-long sliver had been gouged. The gouge was just the sort of shape that might have been made by someone removing a piece with a parrot-beak *Zinke*.

During two summers of digging, the Meiendorf camp—a site used only twice—yielded a total of 345 flint implements, along with the bones and antlers of 105 reindeer, heaped in two piles that had been built up presumably over the course of two seasons. Many of the bones had been split for marrow, and most of the antlers had been gouged for slivers to make pins, needles and a particularly effective spear point, barbed like a harpoon. Thanks to this point, which could not slip from a wound no matter how much the animal thrashed about, the Meiendorf peoples were able to feed themselves efficiently. By counting the antlers and bones in the larger of the two piles, the archaeologists estimated that the hunters killed 72 reindeer during one of their visits. And since the hunters could have camped at Meiendorf only during the warm summer months—at most for a total of 120 days—they must have had something like half a reindeer a day to eat on every day of their stay.

In the wake of Rust's discovery many similar campsites were uncovered in the same region, proving that roving bands of hunters regularly came north in summer to hunt near the glacier's edge. The most fascinating site—with multiple levels of occupation that extended some 4,000 to 5,000 years later than the one at Meiendorf—turned up only a half mile away at a place called Stellmoor. It lay on the shore of another prehistoric lake that is now a bog, and it too was excavated by Rust. Careful digging revealed

that around 12,000 years ago it was occupied regularly over a period of perhaps 30 years and that its occupants still hunted with barbed spears, still had a venison-dominated diet, still sheltered themselves under reindeer-hide tents, still practised the rite of sacrificing the choicest young doe of their first hunt by tossing it into the lake.

But, though much was the same, there were also improvements. Whereas it has not been established beyond a doubt that the Meiendorf hunters had bows and arrows, the evidence that the Stellmoor people did is incontrovertible. More than 100 well-preserved pinewood arrows have been taken from the Stellmoor bog, several of them almost a yard long. Some arrowheads are no more than whittled points, while others consist of a separate flint securely mounted on the shaft. Another indication of the hunters' growing sophistication was a new type of shafted axe whose handle was a curved section of reindeer antler —a shape so efficient for chopping that it is repeated in most axes today. Sometimes the blade was simply a tine of the antler itself, sharpened to a cutting edge; sometimes a flint blade was attached to the tine, or fitted into a groove.

Equipped with antler axes and with bows and arrows, the Stellmoor people undoubtedly found it much easier to contend with the uncertainties of nature. On the evidence of one particular object taken from the Stellmoor bog, they may also have arrived at a much more interesting accommodation with the supernatural. This object appears to be a totem pole, the world's oldest by far. It consists of a seven-foot-long wooden shaft pointed at one end, apparently so it could be driven into the ground. The skull of a reindeer buck is mounted on the other end, and from the

Migrating Scandinavian reindeer move restlessly through the mists of the tundra. In prehistoric times, herds such as this were trailed by hunters for whom the animals meant life itself—food, clothing, shelter and tools.

skull rises a particularly splendid set of antlers. What purpose this object served can only be surmised. Perhaps it stood in the centre of the camp like a guardian spirit, symbolically imbuing the members of the community with the buck's strength; perhaps it played a rôle in some sort of ritual connected with the hunt or with fertility—or both. In any case, it suggests that the Stellmoor people identified the reindeer's spirit with their particular band or community.

Eventually the Stellmoor hunters gave up their annual visits to their lakeside camp—perhaps for more productive hunting elsewhere. Meantime, however, other hunting bands had followed in the wake of the slowly retreating glacier, entering Scandinavia itself; evidence of their occupation, sparse though it is, shows that by 10,000 B.C. one group had settled at a place called Bromme on what is today the large Danish island of Zealand, and that another had reached Sweden, across the way, to camp at Segebro. While alternating between warm and cool periods, the climate in these areas had grown steadily milder. Open forests of birch, ash, pine and aspen now dotted once-hostile sections of northern Europe, and animals other than reindeer had moved in: elk, red deer, beaver, bear and wolverine.

As temperatures climbed higher over the next 2,000 years, more and more trees appeared on the northern landscape. In time, most of southern Scandinavia was covered by coniferous forests. With every passing year the glacier lying on top of the heart of Scandinavia gave up a little more land to the sun. Its retreat accelerated, averaging in some areas about 300 yards annually. By 8000 B.C. southern Sweden and most of western Norway were ice-free; 50 years later the ice had pulled back from the entire coast to the moun-

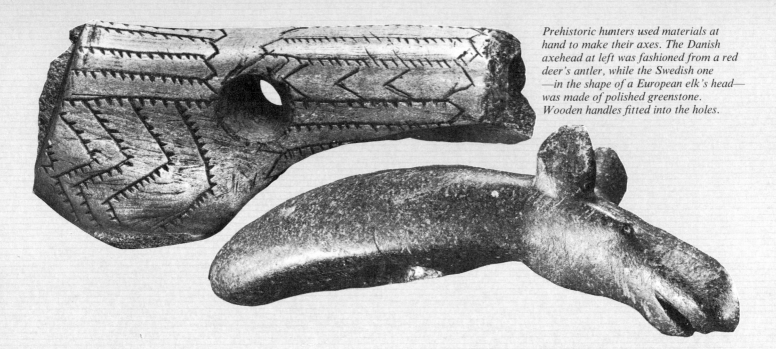

Prehistoric hunters used materials at hand to make their axes. The Danish axehead at left was fashioned from a red deer's antler, while the Swedish one —in the shape of a European elk's head— was made of polished greenstone. Wooden handles fitted into the holes.

tains and uplands of the interior; in another 1,000 years it had all but disappeared, clinging only to the northern mountain peaks.

With this retreat the sea level rose, but so did much of the land, shaping a Scandinavia very different from the one that exists today. As late as 6500 B.C. the Baltic Sea was an inland lake, cut off from the Atlantic by Sweden, which was attached to what is now Germany. Europe's northern coast stretched in an unbroken line from Denmark's Jutland peninsula to the British Isles, and the area now covered by the North Sea was virtually dry land (*pages 20-21*).

So many elemental changes were bound to affect profoundly the lives of the northern European reindeer hunters. The rising sea levels that came with the melting of the ice forced them to abandon many of their traditional hunting grounds. At the same time the advancing forests dramatically altered the environment, forcing the reindeer to move elsewhere. Either the hunters could continue their age-old dependence on the herds and follow them northwards into the Arctic, or the bands could remain in the newly forested land and adapt to it—with all the changes in tools, weapons and hunting techniques that this option would entail.

Accustomed to cold, and to moving on, they no doubt continued to trail the reindeer northwards year after year. By 8000 B.C. their campsites were scattered throughout southwestern Sweden and reached to within 100 miles of the Arctic Circle in Norway. Many of these sites lie along the coast. But instead of still being at sea level, they are now perched about 100 feet above the current shoreline—an index to how much the land rose once the enormous weight of the ice no longer pressed down on it. Some of the sites also lie inland, on the moors of Norway's southern plateau. One of the largest is in direct line with the land bridge that connected Sweden and Denmark in the days when the Baltic was an inland lake—suggesting the route the reindeer hunters may first have taken into the new environment.

Most archaeologists call these early inhabitants of Norway and western Sweden the Fosna people—a name derived from the Fosna peninsula, halfway up the coast of Norway. Though the Fosna settlements were widely scattered over a sizeable area, their inhabitants pursued a common way of life. In summer they pitched their tents near reindeer feeding grounds, on the upland plateaux, and continued to depend on venison for sustenance. In winter they shifted to the coast and established camps along the shore. Here they tapped the sea for an alternate source of food. Then, as now, the Norwegian waters teemed with marine life of every kind—whales, seals, salmon and cod. Sea birds by the thousands nested on the rocky cliffs. Shellfish in a never-ending supply were exposed by the tides. Even with the simplest sort of trap or hook and line it was possible to reap an abundant harvest. Not surprisingly, the Fosna people fished as much as they hunted.

But they were not the only early Scandinavians to do so. Nor were they the first. Far to the north, along the coast of the Arctic Ocean—where the weather can be wintry even in mid-July—another group of intrepid reindeer hunters had moved in and settled down on a fringe of open coastline. Their place of origin is a puzzle. Perhaps they trekked westwards along the coast from the polar areas of Russia, or they may have followed the eastern edge of the receding glacier northwards from Poland through Finland. The best guess is that they arrived sometime before 8000 B.C. and that the reason for their presence in such a forbidding landscape was, once again, the reindeer. But the location of their camps, along the water's edge, suggests that they too were dependent on the sea for a good part of their food. In fact, when the waters along Norway's north coast grew too warm to support seals, around 2000 B.C., the arctic hunters' ancient way of life died out.

Archaeologists label these arctic peoples the Komsa culture for Mount Komsa in northern Norway where the first evidence of their existence was discovered in 1925. Not much remains of it after 100 centuries or so of fierce winds and arctic storms, but there are some truly remarkable rock drawings, or engravings, that are believed to be of Komsa origin. Curiously, they lie at some distance from the campsites. The drawings consist of polished outlines, generally about one inch wide, which may have been done by rubbing the rock with wet sand applied with a piece of wood. Almost without exception the pictures show naturalistically rendered animals—deer, bear, elk, whales, seals—and many are life-sized or even larger. Some are as long as 20 or 30 feet, and each was executed in one continuous line. Either the artists were marvellously skilful or they sketched each picture lightly on the rock to guide themselves in producing the finished drawing.

The Komsa drawings are the oldest in Scandinavia; the fact that they should occur so far north raises some interesting questions. Did the practice of putting pictures on rocks travel south from the rugged Arctic to the relatively benign climate of central and southern Scandinavia where most of the later drawings show up? No one knows. Nor is it known what purpose the pictures served, though it is safe to guess that they involved some sort of hunting magic. Like the famous Cro-Magnon cave paintings of France and Spain, these drawings are often in out-of-the-way places. Some, for instance, have been found on the faces of cliffs over which the bands could have driven their prey, a hunting practice that goes back to Neanderthal times.

Compared to the Komsa drawings, those found elsewhere in Scandinavia tend to be small in scale —some pictures are only a few inches high—and much more detailed. While the northern artists worked mostly in outline, the southern artists often filled their pictures in with linear designs. Some of the designs seem to indicate muscles, hide or internal organs. Others appear to be stylized renderings of a motif common to much primitive art: the so-called life line, which runs from the animal's mouth to the region of his heart. The line presumably stands

A Stone Age Picture Gallery

On exposed cliffs and rock faces in Scandinavia, often far from dwelling sites, Stone Age hunters carved hundreds of animals and fish —and occasionally people—scouring smooth, deep furrows into soft rock and tapping or pricking the designs on harder rock. The practice seems to have begun around 5000 B.C.—perhaps to encourage good hunting—and to have continued for about another 4,000 years. The earliest carvings, located mainly in northern Norway, are naturalistic. Later ones are more complex and symbolic, and many of the animals have life lines running from the muzzle to the heart or lungs, suggesting the areas of greatest vulnerability.

The outlines of an elk dominate a steep escarpment at Drammen in Norway. One explanation for the placement of such carvings is that they marked the cliffs over which hunters drove animals to their deaths on the rocks below.

A human figure, his horned headdress probably marking him as a shaman, seems to be skiing down a rock face at Roedoey in Norway. The bent-tip skis, resembling modern designs, are suited for cross-country travel.

A carved jumble of elk, reindeer and fish covers a cliff at Skogervn in Norway. All the animals have life lines, delineating vital organs, while the fish at the lower right is covered with lines that clearly suggest its scales.

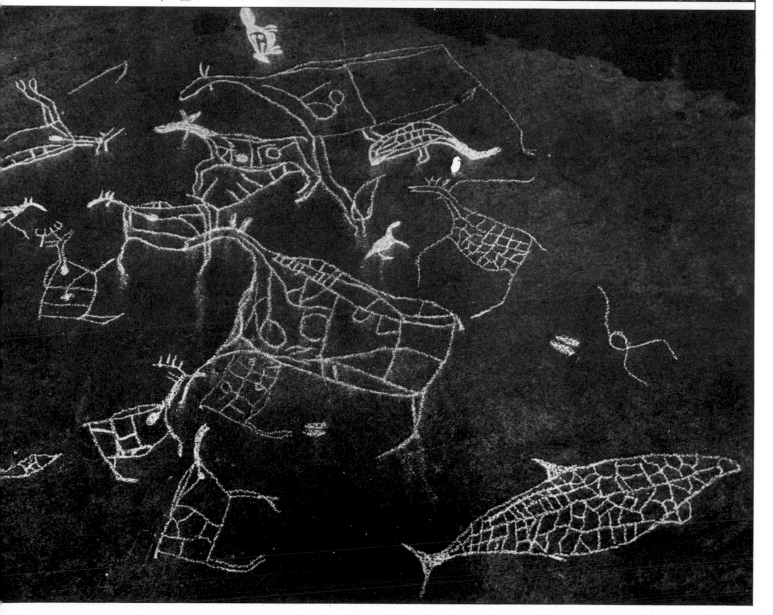

for the animal's vital force and, at the same time, de-lineates the most effective target on the animal's body for the hunter's arrows.

Apart from what they reveal about the hunters themselves, the Stone Age rock drawings also provide glimpses of a new form of transportation appropriate to the Northlands: the ski. What is more, the prehistoric ski seems to have been made in two basic types still used today. One type appears in a Komsa drawing of a little figure wearing long skis (*page 43*) ideally suited for cross-country travel. In another Komsa drawing, a skier wears short, stubby skis similar to those still worn in the north—all the way from Norway clear across the Soviet Union to the Bering Strait and Japan's Hokkaido Island. Broad, with a square back and a tapering toe, the stubby arctic ski is not meant for speed so much as for moving silently over hard-packed snow in pursuit of game. Modern versions often are padded on the bottom with hairy skins to muffle sound. Scandinavian Stone Age hunters, too, probably knew this trick.

In addition to the ski, the ancient Northmen may also have employed the sledge, since the two modes of transportation are similar—and indeed, the sledge would have been even more useful than the ski, making it easier for a hunter to haul home his kill. No rock carvings in Sweden or Norway show sledges; but just across the Baltic, in Finland, several sledge runners have turned up in bogs. The oldest runner, dating back to roughly 7000 B.C., measures some 10 feet long. It curves slightly upwards at the tip, and for much of its length the top of the runner is hollowed out, creating flanged edges along both sides. Holes are drilled through these flanges at intervals. Presumably thongs or cords of rawhide were passed through the holes to lash this runner, and its mate, to the main body of the sledge.

Despite such advantages as sledges and skis, the life style of these northern hunters remained essentially unchanged for thousands of years. Archaeologists think that the Fosna peoples inhabited western Norway until about 3000 B.C. and that the Komsa peoples lingered on for another 1,000 years or so. The standard tool kit of both groups contained the same implements used by their forebears for countless generations: hand axes, scrapers, burins for boring and stone blades for cutting. The stone blades were hardly of the best quality: the Fosna people used low-grade flint; the Komsa people made do with quartz and quartzite, neither of which was a particularly satisfactory material.

Meanwhile, for their contemporaries at the southern end of the Scandinavian peninsula the conditions of life had changed dramatically. What had once been tree-dotted tundra was now covered with expanses of birch and pine. Only here and there did the woods open to the sunlight, revealing a lake or river or marshy clearing. None of the hunters who lived in these forests could have known that there had been a time when this same land was covered with low-growing vegetation or that herds had once grazed where elk and red deer now dodged among the trees.

The first-discovered campsite of these woodland hunters was dug up in 1900 on Zealand, at a place called Maglemose—"great bog" in Danish. Since then the term Maglemose has been applied to a whole culture that extended from eastern Britain, across Denmark and Sweden, to Finland and Estonia on the eastern shores of the Baltic Sea. Much of the North Sea was then of course dry land—part of a land mass

GEAR TO HARVEST THE WATERS

Though forest animals made up a large part of their diet, the Maglemose people, who inhabited Scandinavia from about 8000 B.C. to 4000 B.C., exploited to the full the abundance of fish in their lakes and streams. The archaeological evidence consists of skilfully made hooks, which have been found frequently at Maglemose sites, along with the discarded bones of the fish themselves. Skulls of pike, a species of fish particularly common in northern waters, have turned up with the hooks still in them.

This 32-inch-long section of a simple but effective Maglemose fish trap, from the island of Zealand, was made from pliable willow twigs bound with twine. The fish crowded into such traps through a relatively narrow opening and probably were prevented from escaping by sharp spikes that faced into the interior at the entrance.

Fishhooks—all carved of bone or antler except the small one shaped from grey slate (bottom left)—chart changes in style and shape throughout the Maglemose period. The earliest are small, about one inch long, and are carved in an uninterrupted curve. Later the hooks become larger and, more important, acquire barbs, which both secure the bait and prevent the hook from slipping. The double-pointed hook (bottom right) is a gorge —first used by Cro-Magnons and still used by Eskimos today. Both points embed themselves in the fish's throat.

that extended from Ireland almost to Copenhagen —so that a Maglemose woodland hunter living on the present peninsula of Jutland could have walked to England to visit his Maglemose relatives without getting his feet wet. And by the same token, a good many of the Maglemose campsites, like those of some of the early reindeer hunters, must now lie under the shifting sands of the ocean's floor.

After the displacement of the reindeer by the encroaching forests, the woodland hunters turned to other game, much of it quite small. Occasionally an aurochs, the ancestor of modern cattle, would come crashing through the woods. The record of one day's adventure with such a beast was uncovered in 1905 in a Danish peat bog at Vig, near Jyderup on Zealand, by a group of peat cutters. Apparently the hunters had succeeded in wounding the animal, only to lose it when it plunged into a lake and swam beyond their reach. There the wounded aurochs died and sank. For nearly 10,000 years its bones lay on the bottom, as the lake gradually turned into a bog. But the flint arrowhead that killed him was never displaced; it was still in the skeleton when the peat cutters spotted it. Lodged in the aurochs' seventh rib, the

arrowhead had probably pierced the animal's lung.

From bits and pieces of evidence taken from other bogs a fairly detailed picture can be assembled of the woodland hunters' lives. Though the hunters were essentially nomads, roaming through the woods in search of game, they usually settled down for the summer months at places where the hunting and fishing were particularly good. More often than not they camped in the open, preferably along the shores of a river or a lake.

At one site near Ulkestrup on Zealand, they chose to camp on an island in a small lake. Probably the water between the island and the mainland was shallow enough for wading and the location was ideal for fishing. On the island they built a dwelling, the remains of which came to light in the 1940s during an archaeological dig. The ground plan shows that it was a hut roughly 20 feet long by 15 feet wide, with a doorway facing on the lake. Nothing survived of the walls; probably they were made of perishable rushes and reeds woven together. But pieces of the supporting posts were still in place, and so was some of the flooring laid over the earth to keep out the damp —strips of birchbark almost an inch thick. A five-foot-wide hearth dominated the centre of the hut, and traces of bracken and pine boughs suggest that they were used as bedding. Hazelnut shells littered the floor, indicating either that the hunters were untidy housekeepers or that before breaking camp in the autumn they had gathered and hulled a supply of nuts to carry with them on the trail for use when they needed quick, nourishing food.

The woodland hunters had tools and weapons that were clearly superior to those of the reindeer hunters. They used a flint axe, for example, sturdy enough to chop down trees and a flint knife whose blade made it possible for them to carve some remarkably intricate shapes. At Ulkestrup, the site of the fishermen's hut, archaeologists found a beautifully crafted hazelwood paddle, about four feet long. The boat for which it was made is gone, but dugouts have turned up at other Maglemose sites, and considering the availability of trees, the Ulkestrup boat, too, must have been a dugout canoe.

A second example of Maglemose wood carving—if anything, even more impressive than the hazelwood paddle—was retrieved from another Danish bog, called Holmegaard. It is a long bow, thick and strong at the grip, tapering to slender, springy ends. Its resilience must have made it a truly fine weapon, strong enough to bring down a deer, accurate enough to pick off a bird. The refuse of the woodland hunters regularly contains bird bones.

Along with such aids as boats and paddles and bows and arrows, Maglemose hunters also had help in their food gathering from another quarter. They were regularly accompanied on their hunts by dogs. The canines lived with them in camp; the marks of their teeth can be seen on bones that were tossed onto the camp's refuse pile. And though the dogs may not have been pets, undoubtedly they were permanent members of the hunting band—moving on with it to new campsites, depending upon it for food in a mutually useful arrangement. Dogs eat many of the same foods men do, and the hunting styles of men and dogs also complement each other. With its keen sense of smell, its stamina and its vocalizing during the chase, the dog helped the Maglemose hunter to locate his quarry and run it down for the kill. (In a study done several years ago among African Bushmen of the Kalahari Desert, Canadian anthropologist Richard B. Lee found that a single Bushman hunting with a pack of dogs brought in three times as much meat as six Bushmen hunting without dogs.)

For these woodland hunters, however, great challenges lay in store. As the Scandinavian climate warmed still further, the northern forests they knew so well began to alter yet again; the birch and pine eventually gave way to dense growths of oak, elm and linden. Equally disturbing, the hunters acquired new neighbours. In the Middle East, and then in Europe, other peoples had already taken the first tentative steps into farming and animal husbandry. Spurred by population pressures, farmers began to enter Scandinavia around 4000 B.C., bringing with them their sheep, cattle and pigs, and their precious wheat and barley seeds. Intruded upon by immigrants, the woodland hunters retreated to the seacoasts and, for a while, pursued their accustomed ways. In time they would disappear, and the farmers, with their new life style, would come to the fore as the dominant peoples of Scandinavia. Where formerly the glaciers had shaped the land, now man would begin to alter the look of the environment.

Sacrifice—and the Northmen's Sacred Pools

Besides building structures for worship, the Northmen turned to the world around them and used small bodies of fresh water as settings for some of their most important sacred rites. Here they made sacrifices to the gods to ensure good fortune.

In time, these ponds, pools and lakes filled with vegetation, and eventually turned into spongy peat bogs. In the bogs certain acids and the absence of air stemmed the growth of the bacteria that ordinarily consume organic matter. Thus, the bogs had preserving powers, and many of the Scandinavians' ritual gifts have survived intact to modern times.

The Northmen's practice of leaving gifts in hallowed inland waters began in the Stone Age. It continued through the Bronze and Iron ages into Viking times. Though the character of the tributes changed over the millennia, one feature persisted: the gifts were always things of value.

In earliest times, animals were the commonest offerings. In the scene at right, hunters sacrifice a doe—the finest deer killed on the first day of the summer hunting season. The purpose of the sacrifice was to invite continued success throughout the season.

Close to their tribe's totem, the head of a buck mounted on a pole, hunters heave the carcass of a doe into a glacial lake. A heavy stone buried in the animal's abdomen will sink the body.

Offerings of Booty in Gratitude for Battle Triumphs

The sanctity of certain bogs persisted throughout the Bronze Age, as did the practice of sacrificing animals. An array of ceremonial weapons and finery has been recovered from that period, suggesting that it was an era of prosperity and peace.

The early Iron Age, though, was not a peaceful time for the Northmen. Archaeological finds bear witness to strife, and particularly to victories won against adversaries native to southern lands.

From about 400 B.C. on, it became the custom of the Northmen to sacrifice booty acquired in battle to the deities who had granted them success. Thus, many of the objects from this period recovered in Scandinavia were weapons and armour made by Celts, German tribesmen and Romans. After victories at sea, the Northmen sacrificed the boats their enemies had come in. All these captured items might have been of use, yet they were donated to the gods.

Four boats—including a craft similar to the one shown at the right—have been discovered in Scandinavia. All had been carried overland before being lowered into holy bodies of inland water.

Iron Age Danes prepare to offer to the gods a boat won in battle. Loaded with a cumbersome cargo of arms and armour taken from enemy warriors, the boat will be sunk in the waters of the sacred bog.

Giving Up a Man to the Gods

By the Third Century B.C., the gods of the north were receiving the most treasured gifts of all: human lives. The Northmen deposited hundreds of people—men, women and children—in their sacred bogs. So many bodies have been recovered in recent years (*pages 147-153*) that it almost seems as though the Northmen understood the extraordinary preservative powers in peat. In any case, they must have felt that a body placed in a bog acquired a kind of immortality.

Doubtless some sacrificial victims were war captives and criminals; others were women accused of adultery, whose bodies were offered as pleas for forgiveness. Some, though, seem to have gone willingly to their deaths, honoured that they were singled out for sacrifice. One of these victims, whose body turned up in 1950, still wears a look of serenity (*page 124*), suggesting that he accepted his fate—like the man in the scene at the right—with calmness, perhaps even gratitude.

A human sacrifice, his hands tied behind his back, stands resignedly as a noose of braided leather is tightened about his neck. Once dead, he will be thrown into the sacred bog, there, presumably, to dwell forever with the spirits.

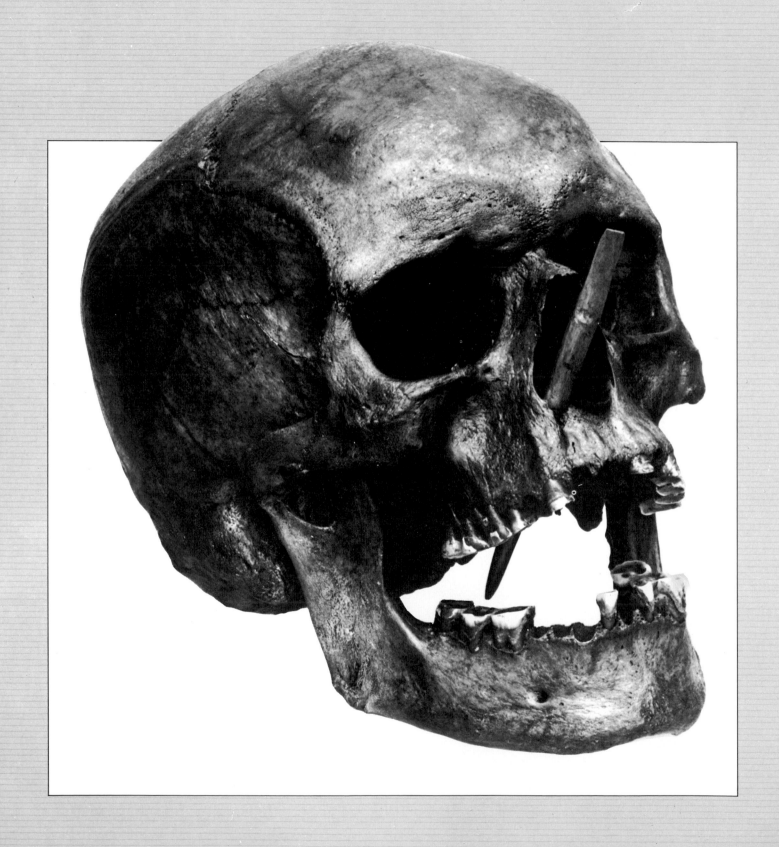

Sometime around 6000 B.C. life changed momentously for the Scandinavian woodland hunters. First, their land was again transformed, both in its expanse and its appearance; and then, less than 2,000 years later, new waves of immigrants into the Northlands introduced the hunters to agriculture. Directly or indirectly, both events were the result of the warming climate. Not only did dense forests of oak, elm and linden overtake the stands of conifers and birch, but the runoff from the melting glacial ice to the north caused the waves to lap higher and higher along the coasts. The rising water washed up the rivers and over the marshlands to create the North Sea. It separated the British Isles from the mainland of Europe and formed Denmark's Jutland peninsula, along with the archipelago of islands that now makes up the other half of that sea-girt kingdom. Mostly the water rose too slowly to be noticed. But there must have been times, too, of storms and high seas when vast areas were inundated and hunting bands fled their campsites hurriedly, never to return.

Forced to live in smaller and smaller areas of land, competing with one another for the dwindling supply of big game, the woodland hunters of the south turned more and more to the waters around them for food. Now they regularly pitched camp along riverbanks and the shore, and fished as well as hunted. They gathered oysters and mussels from the rocks,

A tapered bone arrowhead projects from the skull of a late Stone Age Northman found in a Danish bog. Was he killed and tossed into the bog as a sacrifice—or was he the victim of fighting? Archaeologists do not know, but other skeletons from the same period give evidence of crushing blows to the head, a possible indication of strife between local farmers and newcomers entering Scandinavia from the south.

set nets and traps for silvery cod and herring and spawning salmon, and paddled their dugout canoes along the coast in search of seals, porpoises and the newly laid eggs of sea turtles.

If a coastal campsite proved to be particularly good, in a sheltered cove that offered plenty of food, a roving band might visit it continually for centuries. With each brief residency the hunters would leave behind the telltale evidence of their occupancy: a layer of shells; the bones of fish, birds and beasts; discarded flints; broken pots; the ashes of campfires. Over the centuries their refuse accumulated into huge piles; one measures 900 feet long and six feet deep.

To the latter-day discoverers of these massive shell heaps in Jutland, they seemed at first to be nothing more than ancient oyster beds. Only in the middle of the 19th Century were they properly identified as the work of men, not nature. And the man who identified these so-called kitchen middens was Jens Worsaae, who later succeeded Christian Thomsen as director of Denmark's National Museum.

Kitchen-midden sites have since been located along stretches of the Baltic and North seas. At one Danish site called Meilgaard, archaeologists actually calculated the number of oyster shells the midden contained, and from this estimate they determined the number of years the site had been visited. Using as a base the annual yield of the near-by oyster bed —17,000 oysters—they concluded that a band of 20 people could have camped at Meilgaard 10 days a year, eating six and a half dozen oysters each within that time and that there were enough shells in the midden for this pattern of visits to have been repeated annually for a thousand years.

In returning to the same coastal sites year after

year the midden folk did not seem to mind setting up camp in the midst of the previous year's garbage, perhaps because the piles of shells offered better drainage than the surrounding land. Indeed, some pitched their tents, built their fires and cooked and ate their meals on top of the refuse heaps. Sometimes they even buried their dead among the shells.

Palle Lauring, one of the best-known writers on Scandinavia's prehistory, has supplied a graphic description of what he imagines conditions were like in a kitchen-midden community. He sees the top of the mound itself as "made up entirely of slimy oyster shells, fish guts, offal from gutted game, cods' heads, intestines from birds, fur scrapings and, mixed up in the general mess, various superfluities of the human body. The stench must have been appalling, and in the summer the flies . . . formed a compact, buzzing blue cloud above the heap. It is incomprehensible that anyone survived this astonishing filth."

In such surroundings, Lauring observes, one would hardly expect to find a high level of culture. As artisans the midden people left little to show for themselves. A single four-toothed comb from Meilgaard (*page 58*) indicates at least an interest in grooming. Flint blades—of great thinness and evenness, some 12 inches long—bespeak a skill in toolmaking. Only a few zigzag lines of decoration carelessly scratched on pieces of pottery and bone hint of any degree of artistic concern—and pottery itself came late to the midden folk.

Yet, they did have pottery and that fact in itself is remarkable. It is a crude sort of ware, to be sure, but it is the very first pottery to appear in Scandinavia. The midden potters worked with strips of clay, which they coiled into spirals and pinched together to produce two basic shapes of ware (*page 59*). One was a shallow bowl, rather like the blubber lamps of modern Eskimos, used perhaps for the same purpose. The other was a thick-walled jar with a pointed bottom. This seemingly awkward design was nevertheless functional: wedged into the fire between stones, with charcoal banked up around it, the pot's surface would have received the maximum amount of heat.

In the archaeologists' view of things, any prehistoric people who have learned how to make pottery have taken a significant step forward in their intellectual development. The flintworker, however deft, does little more than reorganize the material at hand. But the potter takes unrelated materials—clay, grit and water—and transforms them into a material that is entirely new. To do this successfully, he has to combine his ingredients in the correct proportions, has to work out a method for building them into the desired shape, has to recognize the importance of heat to the hardening process.

How the knowledge of pottery came to the midden folk, probably no one will ever find out. In any case, it apparently arrived around the time of the first tentative ventures into farming near the end of the Fifth Millennium B.C. The evidence for farming is slight —a few bones of domesticated cattle and sheep, a few impressions of cultivated grains mixed into the clay of pots—but it does signal impending change. Did knowledge of agriculture filter into Scandinavia from stray contacts with neighbouring peoples to the south who in turn had learned from their own, more southerly neighbours? Or was the information brought in by immigrants? No one knows. However, farming arrived, it did not all at once revolutionize the Northmen's lives; instead, it slowly infiltrated their existing culture. Planting and harvesting crops in open patches of forest, caring for sheep and cattle were simply adjuncts to the main business of living, which continued to be hunting and fishing. Extracurricular agricultural activities provided a reserve for hunters who had the foresight to plan ahead for the day when they might run short of game.

Not until around 4000 B.C. did agriculture become a serious venture. This date apparently also marks the founding, by a band numbering perhaps 200, of a settled farming community on what was then an island at the end of a sandspit extending into a bay of the Baltic Sea. Today the island is a landlocked hill on a farm in eastern Jutland, called Barkaer, and around the hill, where the water was, is a peat bog. The first clues to the existence of the ancient settlement were discovered in 1928, but not until 1940 did a young archaeologist at the University of Copenhagen begin to excavate it in earnest. His name was Peter Vilhelm Glob, and he would go on to become the head of Denmark's National Museum.

Since then, the settlement at Barkaer has been thoroughly investigated, and the findings have shed important light on the beginnings not only of farming in Scandinavia but of agriculture in Europe in general. The inhabitants of Barkaer and other, similar groups were the vanguard of a steady northward migration of pioneer farmers. Unlike the indigenous hunter-farmers, who simply planted seeds in forest clearings, the newcomers attacked the forests with axes and fire. Slashing and burning their way through the wilderness, they cleared fields and pastures, used them until the soil was exhausted or the population too large for the land to support it, then moved on.

All across southern Scandinavia the farmers unwittingly wrote the record of their coming in the strata of ancient lake sediments and in peat bogs. But only in the early years of this century did scientists come to realize that the record was there to be read. In the early 1900s, a professor of botany at Stockholm University, Gustav Lagerheim, discovered that peat contained millions of microscopic grains of pollen blown into it from blooming vegetation—thousands of grains in a single one-eighth-inch cube of peat. It was left to a young Swedish geologist, Lennart von Post, to establish in 1916 that pollen samples could be used to construct a picture not just of the vegetation in one area but, through the analyses of many samples from many different places, of an entire prehistoric landscape. His work was revolutionary and pollen analysis is now one of the basic tools of archaeologists the world over.

Pollen grains, as it happens, are the fingerprints of the plant world. Every species of plant produces pollen unique to its species. Moreover, the pollen grains are encased in shells so hard that they are practically indestructible and thus can remain intact for aeons, as when trapped in sediment or peat. By analysing ancient pollen samples under a microscope, Lennart von Post was able to construct tables showing the plant life that flourished in a given region during a particular period of time.

When the pollen collected from the bog at Barkaer was analysed, a series of ecological events became evident. With the coming of the farmers, for instance, the pollen of large trees all but disappeared from the settlement site—indicating that the trees had been cut down. Simultaneously, there was a rise in the pollen of cereal grasses and pasture plants like clover

This two-inch Stone Age bone comb was uncovered in 1849, amid an eight-foot layer of oyster shells, by workmen digging for road-surfacing material on the northeast coast of the Jutland peninsula. The find helped Danish archaeologist Jens Worsaae establish the existence of a kitchen-midden culture.

Both vessels above, a pot and a disc-shaped oil lamp from the kitchen-midden period (5000-2700 B.C.), were made by spiralling long, thin strips of clay and smoothing the surfaces. Working from the top, the craftsmen stretched the pot's base to a point that could be firmly embedded in the embers.

and sorrel, typically associated with farming. But near the close of a 10-year period, the pollen changed again, pointing to the growth of scrub trees such as birch and aspen, which generally spring up where land is abandoned and the forest begins to return.

Looking at this evidence, geologist Johannes Iversen of Denmark's University of Copenhagen drew the obvious conclusion—that the farmers had "cleared large areas of the original forest with axes, burned over the clearings, planted small fields of cereals and used the rest for pasturing animals". But he was curious about the farmers' methods. How had they managed to fell large hardwood trees, such as oak, with stone axes? And once the trees were down, how had they burned off so much timber at once?

To answer these questions Iversen decided to conduct the kind of experiment the Danes excel at: the investigation of the past through its re-creation in the present. In 1950 he obtained permission from the Danish government to clear the trees from a two-acre patch of a national forest; considering how little surviving forest there is in a country as heavily cultivated as Denmark, getting approval was no mean accomplishment. And to help him, in addition to several professional colleagues, he engaged two expert woodcutters. In fact, so keen was Iversen on accuracy that he borrowed a number of Stone Age axes from the National Museum and fitted them with handles that duplicated the originals.

The first efforts of this curious company of loggers came to grief. Swinging in their accustomed style —with long, powerful strokes—the woodcutters succeeded only in chipping or breaking one flint axe after another. Since the woodcutters did not seem to be able to modify their swing, Iversen and his col-

The axe, that basic tool of the Stone Age, underwent important modifications in Scandinavia. The bone-handled Danish axes with stag-antler heads, at left and right, date from 5000 B.C.; the stone axeheads in the panel between them date from around 2000 B.C. When the antler axes were made, bone implements could be shaped and smoothed by rubbing with stones, flint ones only by chipping. The later period's toolmakers, able to grind and polish flint, turned out smooth, thin axeheads, such as the two at right above and the one whose reconstructed haft rests on an axe-tapered log. In a modern experiment, this last type felled an oak 16 inches thick in less than an hour.

leagues took over and, by trial and error, devised their own unconventional technique. Working with short, chopping strokes, involving mostly their wrists and forearms, they downed oak trees as much as 12 inches thick in less than half an hour. One man even used the same flint-axe blade, a blade that had not been sharpened since the Stone Age, throughout the entire clearing operation without having to pause once to resharpen it.

Iversen and his colleagues felled the larger trees as modern lumberjacks do, by cutting wedges in either side of the trunks to control their fall. They tackled the smaller trees by cutting around the trunk, beaver fashion. And foreseeing that parallel lines of fallen trees would be easier to deal with than a tangle of trunks and branches, they dropped all the trees in the same direction. Thus, at the completion of their woodcutting, they had a two-acre field of toppled trees, all pointing north and south.

To fire the trunks Iversen used a method that has persisted in rural Finland for many centuries. A blanket of brushwood about 30 feet long was laid along one edge of the clearing and fired with birchbark torches staked into the brush at intervals. When the first row of trunks was burning well, it was rolled with the aid of long poles against the next row. Thus, each subsequent row was fired until, in three or four days, one entire acre was reduced to ashes. The second acre of felled trees was not burned, but simply cleared to serve as a control for the phase of the experiment that followed.

One of Iversen's colleagues, Axel Steensberg, an expert on agricultural methods, planted ancient varieties of wheat and barley by spreading the seeds on both the burned and the unburned clearings, and then raking them into the ground with a forked branch. Predictably the burned field, because of the fertilizing wood ash, produced a luxuriant crop. Indeed, the scientists were surprised to see just how lush the growth was in the first season. In contrast, because of the acidic soil, the grain grew hardly at all in the unburned field. More important, however, the two fields were allowed to lie fallow for one year after they had become exhausted and in that time they produced two different kinds of vegetation. In the unburned field the plants that appeared were essentially the same ones that had been there before —bracken ferns, grasses and sedges. But the burned field produced a whole new set of plants: daisies, thistle, dandelion, mosses and plantain, sometimes referred to as the farmer's footprint, since it appears only where soil has been under cultivation. In time there also appeared in the burned field many of the very same kinds of scrub trees—birch, aspen, linden and hazel—that had been noted in the pollen samples taken from the bog at Barkaer.

One can safely assume that the hunters resented any intrusion on their domain. Prowling through the forests near the farmers' encampments, the wary hunters would have heard for the first time the sound of falling timber and seen the smoke rising from the burning clearings. Soon the effect these activities had on their already diminishing game supply inevitably must have caused anger, and relations between the two groups must have grown at least strained and perhaps even hostile. Certainly the 200 farming people who arrived at Barkaer around 4000 B.C. thought they had something to fear or they would not have selected for their settlement a site surrounded on three

The First Scandinavian Designs

The farmers who began to enter Scandinavia from the south around 4000 B.C. apparently brought with them both the notion of a mother goddess, whose eyes gaze from the pottery fragment at right, and a southern sense of decoration. Potters achieved their textures and patterns simply—by scratching the clay with pointed implements and with the edges of mussel shells, and by pressing it with twisted cords as on the shard at bottom left. Their designs still influence Scandinavian potters.

This graceful, lug-handled bowl is Denmark's finest piece of prehistoric pottery.

Incised and pressed-in patterns richly ornament a perfect specimen of a broad-brimmed pedestal vase found in a Danish bog.

A massive capstone appears to float on top of the upright supports of a dolmen, or grave monument, in Aamosen, Denmark. Nearly 5,000 Stone Age dolmens (the word comes from the Breton meaning "table rocks") have been mapped in Denmark; approximately 1,800 still stand.

sides by water and connected to the mainland only by a narrow sandspit.

When they first arrived at Barkaer, the newcomers no doubt sheltered themselves in skin tents and rough lean-tos of branches and twigs. Huddled anxiously around their campfires, with the dark, unknown forest so close by and an occasional sharp warning bark from their dogs alerting them to danger, they had to wonder—as has every group of pioneers before and since—about the wisdom of leaving their old land for a new one. But gradually, as they went about the business of clearing the forest and planting their seeds, they adjusted to Barkaer and began to construct permanent dwellings.

The buildings at Barkaer occupied almost the whole of the tiny island, which was only some 200 yards square. They consisted of two long houses laid out parallel to each other, with a broad cobblestone street, approximately 30 feet wide, running between them. Dark circles in the sand—traces of what once were posts and stakes—give some idea of what the houses looked like. The posts ran down the middle of each dwelling to support the roof and also around the perimeter of the house at regular intervals to brace the walls. The stakes, set about eight inches apart, formed the walls themselves as well as the inner partitions or room dividers; they must have been laced with branches and twigs to keep out the wind, rain and snow. Stones placed along the outer walls helped shore them up, and it was from the rectangular arrangement of these stones that archaeologists first deduced the buildings' shape and size.

When constructing their dwellings, the farmers apparently took out a kind of insurance to safeguard the group's future welfare. In two of the postholes they buried a treasure, probably an offering to a household god. The treasure consisted of 50 amber beads, a small clay flask and two tiny copper pendants. The latter must have been treasure indeed, for copper did not begin to enter Scandinavia in any appreciable quantities until about 2,000 years later.

Although life must have been hard at Barkaer, the farmers seem to have flourished, for they expanded the two houses at least once. Initially, both measured about 260 feet long and 20 feet wide (one house was slightly wider than the other) and each was divided at 12-foot intervals into rooms, or apartments, that served as the living quarters of single families. But as Barkaer's population increased, more rooms were added to the ends of both houses. At the settlement's height the dwellings held 52 families, a population equivalent to that of a modern Danish township.

With a foothold in the new land established, the Barkaer farmers settled into a round of activities apparently not too different from those of any rural European community right down to the 20th Century. In the morning, the men crossed the narrow sand causeway with their animals to pasture them and to tend the fields; at twilight they trudged home, driving their cattle and sheep before them. Some archaeologists think that the broad paved thoroughfare between the Barkaer houses was actually a corral, in which the people penned their livestock at night to protect them from predators.

While the men busied themselves with the hard work of farming, the women of Barkaer engaged in such essential tasks as making clothing, grinding grain on rough stone slabs and shaping clay into an astonishing array of pots. To judge from the number of potsherds scattered over the floors of their dwell-ings, the farmers seem to have required a constant supply of vessels. Some were used for cooking and eating, some for storing the end products of their labours—grain, milk, perhaps even beer. The pots ranged in size and shape from squat cups to elegant tall-necked urns called beakers, which incidentally provided archaeologists with the identifying label for the people of this period: the Funnel-Neck Beaker culture. Often the pots were decorated with geometric patterns of dots and lines. Clearly the potters took pride in their work and considered the pots to be more than simply utilitarian objects, although they were certainly that too. Archaeologists consider them among the finest pots ever produced in Scandinavia (*pages 62-63*).

Similarly, the tools and weapons of these pioneer farmers were advanced well beyond those of the hunters. Unlike the midden folk, whose flint tools still bore the chip marks of the flaking process, the farmers spent long hours grinding and polishing their axes with sand and water until the surface of the stone was as smooth as the inner bark of a tree. The result of this patient work was a sturdier tool that chipped less because its surface was unfaceted. But the farmers must also have been aware that in polishing their tools they were making them more beautiful—and more like the new metal tools that people in other parts of Europe had already begun to use.

Archaeologists refer to this period as the Neolithic Age, or New Stone Age, and in Scandinavia it produced some distinctive tool types. One of the most important was the flint axe, the implement with which the farmers cleared the forests. The axeheads found in Denmark, southern Sweden and Norway take various forms and reach what a number of archaeologists believe to be the peak of the neolithic toolmaker's art. Early examples are oval in cross section, with curved blades and pointed butts like modern pick-axes. Later examples are patterned after metal prototypes and are rectangular in cross section and very long, some measuring as much as 18 inches. Still later versions are square in cross section, with thick butts and short, straight blades.

The farmers seem to have used their axes only for the intended purpose—cutting wood. But the presence at a few farming sites of another kind of implement, called a dagger-axe, raises an interesting question: just what was it used for? The dagger-axe was made of a stone dagger mounted at right angles to a wooden handle, and in appearance it resembled a tomahawk. As several experts in stone tools have pointed out, its design would make it seem better suited for combat between men than for hunting. (With good reason, hunters preferred to bring down their prey from afar, using spears or bows and arrows.)

The new farmers in Scandinavia obviously needed to defend themselves. They possessed both food and goods that doubtless attracted marauders and covetous neighbours. As the Danish writer Palle Lauring has put it, "At the hunters' settlement there was nothing to be had but women; stocks of food were rarely so large as to be worth the risk. To dispossess the farmer of his cultivated soil and to slay the herdsman and take possession of his livestock were obvious temptations. With the farmer and herdsman came war, war with simple motives and on a much greater scale than the occasional small feuds between hunting tribes."

But despite the risk of bloodshed, the farmers continued to push northwards. By 3200 B.C. they had settled all through Denmark, and were established on the Scandinavian peninsula as far north as Oslo. Sometimes they remained only a few years; at other times they occupied one spot for several generations. No doubt what limited the length of their stay was the diminishing fertility of the soil, although at Barkaer there was apparently a second compelling reason for leaving.

Archaeologists believe that the Barkaer farmers had a serious problem with drifting sand. With the felling of the trees along the shore, thick roots no longer helped hold the beach in place. Over a 10-year span blowing sand found its way through the walls of houses and raised the floor levels by as much as 20 inches, lowering the headroom accordingly in rooms that must have had low ceilings to begin with. At any rate, after at most two decades, Barkaer was abandoned to the drifting sands—and it is, of course, precisely because of its sandy covering that the settlement was so well preserved.

With the spread of farming throughout southern Scandinavia came a more settled way of life, but it was a life fraught with new anxieties. Too much sun could parch the fields, too much rain could drown them. Predators might creep in at night and slaughter the sheep, and diseases might strike the cattle. Planted too early, a seed failed to send up a shoot. Harvested too late, the grain would rot in the fields. It was all mysterious and incomprehensible, and after the farmers had done all they could of planting and hoeing and tending their crops, there was nothing for them to do but to trust to the favour of nature.

In their dependence on forces beyond their control, the farmers seem to have developed a deep

concern with religion and the hereafter. The evidence is plain to see: the stone monuments and burial mounds that dot the southern Scandinavian landscape today. Indeed, the presence of a stone burial chamber near Barkaer is what first attracted P. V. Glob, the young archaeology student, to the site. When the midden people buried their dead, they sometimes wrapped them in tree-bark shrouds before depositing them in their shell heaps; and on occasion they covered the bodies with stones either to keep dogs and other animals out or spirits in. But the farmers came along and went much further. No longer constantly on the move, they could afford to give their honoured dead burials in elaborate stone structures that attest to not only their religious sense but also their engineering skills and the growing importance of communal efforts.

Most of these monuments are of a type known as dolmens. They once numbered 5,000 in Denmark alone, and nearly 1,800 still survive there. The oldest, dating to 4200 B.C., consist of three or four glacial boulders, topped by truly mammoth capstones (*page 64*). Inside there is generally room for only one body—curled up—and a few token grave goods: perhaps a stone axe for a man, a few amber beads for a woman. Often built on mounds of earth, the dolmens themselves were covered by heaped-up earth. Many of the hillocks thus created were surrounded by rectangular stone fences that may represent an attempt to duplicate the ground plan of the farmers' multi-family dwellings. The farmers themselves may well have regarded the dolmens as houses of the dead. But the dead who occupied them must have been special members of the community. Presumably the dolmens were built for elders or leaders as reminders of their greatness, and perhaps also as places of worship where later generations could come to commune with the spirits of wise ancestors.

In time, there appeared a second kind of monument called a passage grave. Apparently introduced by yet another wave of farmers from the south, it never found wide favour and seems to have been built over a span of only one or two generations. Unlike the dolmen, the passage grave was intended for multiple burials and accordingly was much bigger; some held as many as a hundred bodies. This grave, too, was made of glacial boulders, which formed the walls, topped by immense capstones. The entire grave, except for the capstones, was covered with earth to form a large mound. In Denmark alone there are more than 700 passage graves, in Sweden more than 300, and they continued to be used by later peoples for the interment of their own dead, right through the Bronze Age.

As its name implies, the passage grave was entered through a narrow tunnel; in fact, some tunnels are so constricted that visitors would have had to crawl in on all fours. Inside, however, there is usually a spacious room, round or rectangular in shape. Cool, damp and smelling of earth, such a chamber resembles nothing so much as a cave. Indeed, there is speculation that the cave was its architectural antecedent. People may well have assembled in the passage graves for ceremonies; in any case, they must have visited the graves routinely to leave offerings of food and drink in clay vessels, for some of the entrances are littered with thousands and thousands of potsherds. The custom continued until quite recently; Scandinavian country people deposited similar offerings at the mouths of the tombs. One Danish ex-

cavator recalls that a passage grave on one farmer's land was visited regularly, every Christmas, by the farmer's wife, who left a bowl of porridge for "the giants and the spirit that dwelt there".

Considering the size of the dolmens and of the passage graves, and of the massive stones used to build them, it is not surprising that later Scandinavians —while still unaware of the meaning of these monuments—referred to them as giants' graves and trolls' chambers, and believed that their land had once been populated by a race of supermen. Supermen the grave builders were not, but to judge from the work involved, they must have been inspired by a powerful belief. What could this belief have been?

If, like so much else in prehistoric Scandinavia, the concept of the dolmen and the passage grave was an import from the south, then the belief that went with it may also have been an import—involving the worship of a mother goddess, a great fertility figure whom the first farmers of the Middle East had venerated several thousand years earlier and whose cult eventually spread to Europe. (It may well be her eyes that gaze out from fragments of clay vessels found in some of the burial chambers.) Interestingly, women's ornaments predominate over all other objects recovered from Danish passage graves, suggesting that women may have been at the head of a particular clan or tribe, or were revered because of their innate connection with the life-giving forces of nature.

Whatever the significance of the monuments, they survive today as moving reminders of the prehistoric Scandinavian farmers' attempt—in the face of so much that was beyond human control—to offset their own brief mortality by leaving behind something that would endure for the ages.

Mysteries from the Bronze Age

One of the most tantalizing heritages bestowed upon modern scholars by Bronze Age Northmen are the thousands of carvings that appear on the rock outcroppings of central and southern Scandinavia. Although it is known that they were done throughout the Bronze Age, who made them —priest or layman—and why remains as much a mystery as the origins of the earlier Stone Age rock drawings of northern Scandinavia (*page 42*).

Seen to their best advantage at dawn or sunset, when the low sun fills the shallow outlines with dark shadows, the carvings are so cryptic in their symbolism and diverse in their subject matter that, in the total absence of written records, scholars can do little more than speculate upon their meanings. It seems likely that the carvings were incised piecemeal, without any regard to artistic grouping, perhaps in the course of religious ceremonies. Indeed, many of the motifs that are reproduced here and on the following pages—supersized male figures, ploughs, exaggerated genitalia —seem to suggest a fertility cult associated with agriculture.

The subjects that recur most frequently in rock carvings are the Northmen's high-prowed ships. Here, a veritable flotilla sails amid many different figures, including a man spearing an animal (upper left) and an antlered elk (centre).

This strange maypole-like object with three figures cavorting around it may record part of a spring rite. Experts believe the oval shape in the corner (lower right)—seen as the outline of a footprint—signifies the presence of a divine being who, perhaps because of a taboo, was shown only symbolically. Found in many carvings, such footprints come singly or in pairs, shod or unshod.

In carvings found on Sweden's west coast, a group of male figures engage in seemingly unrelated activities: while one blows a kind of trumpet, or lur (upper left), another brandishes an axe (upper right) and a third holds a bow (bottom right). The round shape at top right is thought to be a sun disc, a motif that appears often in such carvings.

A Northman guides a primitive plough pulled by two oxen in this rock carving on the face of an ice-smoothed cliff on the western coast of Sweden. The obvious symbolism of turning over a field for spring planting suggests that the carving might have been executed as part of a fertility cult.

Domesticated animals—like the bull at right, trailed by another—appear frequently among the rock carvings, demonstrating the preoccupation of Bronze Age Northmen with sedentary farming life. Above the bulls are two manned ships and a reindeer. Most of the carvings have been found on rock surfaces facing south or east, never far from water supplies or fertile soil, where presumably the fruits of the Northmen's husbandry might flourish.

Chapter Four: Taking to the Waters

By the time the Vikings set sail in their dragon vessels in the Eighth and Ninth centuries A.D., the Scandinavians were already masters of the waters around them, with a 4,000-year-old tradition of seafaring. As far back as 3000 B.C. they were plying the coasts of the Baltic and North seas to trade with one another, and their prowess as seamen and boatbuilders undoubtedly contributed to the opening of trade between northern and southern Europe in the years after 2000 B.C.

One glance at a map explains why this should have been so. In Denmark, for instance, no one lives more than 40 miles from the sea, and the land itself is divided by narrow straits and channels into 600 islands. In Norway and Sweden the situation is much the same. Hardly a person in either nation lives more than 200 miles from an inlet or fjord. The coastlines of both countries are embellished by a multitude of straits and sheltering coves, while the back country is laced by a network of lakes and rivers.

On these labyrinthine waterways countless generations of Northmen gradually learned the lessons of seamanship, testing and perfecting their skills and techniques. Water became so natural an environment to them that in a sense it entered their lifeblood. Not only did it link them to one another and to the rest of the world, but it was, almost from the start, a constant element in the collective Scandinavian imagination. From the Stone Age, when it was the practice to sacrifice a doe in a glacial lake, to the Iron Age, when human beings were tossed into bogs to please the gods, water seems to have had sacred connotations to the Northmen (*pages 48-53*).

Water was also a means of communication, and in Scandinavia conditions obviously encouraged water travel. Where the terrain was mountainous or the distances great, men instinctively looked ·to the lakes and rivers. In summer they moved along them by raft or dugout; in winter they walked over the frozen, unobstructed surfaces. Boats offered an efficient way of transporting groups of people or quantities of goods. One authority has estimated that it would take 340 pack horses to transport a 34-ton load overland, while the same cargo, moving by water, could easily be carried by one small Scandinavian sloop manned only by two men and a boy.

In building a boat, as in building anything else, the material and the tools used dictate the form of the finished product. Where reeds were abundant, as in Egypt, men made boats of bundled reeds. Where trees were abundant, but men had no axes sturdy enough to fell them, as in some parts of Australia, boats were made of bark sewn together with animal sinews and strengthened with wooden thwarts. The Scandinavian woodland hunters, with their hafted flint axes and their plentiful supply of timber, made their boats of wood. In fact, the availability of good timber throughout much of Scandinavia probably contributed greatly to the region's shipbuilding development. At first, the forests provided the Northmen with logs whose girth was large enough for dugout canoes (*page 74*). Later, as the boatwrights' skill grew, tall, straight trees yielded the long flexible planks

Aboard a 15-foot dugout of a type dating back some 8,000 years, a young Dane paddles past a sister vessel resting in the reeds. Both canoes were made by employing the methods of the ancient Northmen as part of a modern experiment in Stone Age living. Using flint axes to fell oaks, the boatbuilders, ancient and modern, hollowed out the trunks by setting smouldering charcoal in grooves cut lengthways into the wood.

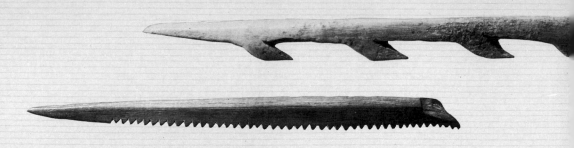

needed to construct vessels that could withstand the buffeting of the open sea.

And yet, it may not have been in a wooden boat that the first Scandinavians went to sea. Long before there was any regular trade and long before there were any farmers, Scandinavians undoubtedly used boats. The earliest Northmen to take to the water were the northern reindeer hunters. Living along the coast of the north Atlantic and Arctic oceans, gazing out to sea, these intrepid bands were apparently tempted by the sight of fat seals, porpoises and whales swimming offshore. By trial and error—which probably included numerous disasters—they learned to build a seaworthy boat. What the boat was made of, no one knows, since there were precious few trees in that part of Scandinavia. But rock carvings in northern Norway depict vessels that look rather like the Eskimos' skin-covered umiak, which is propelled by paddling. And it seems likely that the hunters' first boat was also made of skin, stretched over a lightweight frame of wood.

Like the umiak, this vessel had high sides to deflect sea swells and a steep prow and stern for clearing surf. The rock drawings also show it with the distinctive "ears" of the umiak, fore and aft; the umiak's ears, projections of its wooden frame, are used by Eskimos to drag their boats onto the beach. The ears of the Scandinavian boats may well have served the same purpose.

If the reindeer hunters' boat was indeed an ancient version of the umiak, it must have suited the hunters' way of life ideally. For one thing, an umiak, which can be up to 30 feet long, is large enough to hold a whaling party. For another, its skin can be removed and replaced when the covering is damaged.

Doubtless such features would have appealed to the reindeer hunters. But more important, a skin boat is perfect for use in icy water; though the umiak might seem fragile, its flexible sides can actually absorb the blows of floating chunks of ice better than the rigid sides of a wooden boat.

Chances are that the first seagoing hunters stuck close to land, and they must have paddled anxiously for shore as soon as the wind sprang up and the sea got rough. Nevertheless, their achievement—all things considered—was a far greater one than that of their contemporaries in southern Scandinavia. When the Maglemose hunters of the woodland regions took to the water, they stuck mostly to rivers and lakes. Their purpose was to fish—not to grapple with whales and seals.

What kind of boat did *they* use? Bits and pieces of Maglemose vessels have come to light in northern Europe, the earliest dating back to at least 6000 B.C., and it is clear from the evidence that the boat was a dugout canoe. A dugout, of course, is one of the simplest of crafts to build; so basic is its construction that the techniques vary little from place to place and period to period.

In southern Chile the Alakaluf Indians still make dugouts, and they lead a life in many ways similar to that of prehistoric Scandinavians. They too live in a watery world of islands and intricate coastlines; they depend upon fish and shellfish for food, and they hunt sea lions. Their method of building a boat, observed by anthropologists in the 1950s, must be similar to the method used by the early Scandinavians, and it is therefore worth examining.

The Alakaluf boatbuilder begins by searching the forest for the right kind of tree—a dead beech of suf-

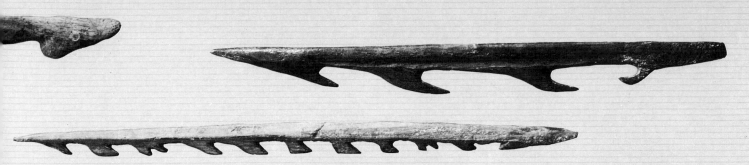

ficient girth. If he is extremely lucky, he may find such a tree close to shore, but ordinarily he has to go several miles inland. When he has found it, he calls on one or two of his friends for assistance, and together they fell the tree and cut off the trunk. Then they begin the job of hollowing it out with their axes, hacking and chipping away at the wood until they have a hull about an inch thick. The ends—to be finished off later—are left somewhat thicker than the rest.

Now that the hull is light enough for the boatbuilders to carry, they clear a path through the woods to the settlement, down at the water's edge; eight or 10 other members of the community join the boatbuilders to help with the portage. At the settlement the hull is further thinned, smoothed and shaped, until the boatbuilders are satisfied with its appearance. In many parts of the world, where dugouts are made of extremely hard wood, such as oak, the boatbuilding process is now complete. But because beech is a relatively soft wood, the Alakaluf Indians' boat undergoes further shaping, designed to widen the hull and increase its interior dimensions.

This step is accomplished by steaming and stretching the wood. Steaming is a common practice among peoples whose dugouts are made of softwoods such as ash, aspen and poplar; in fact, in some parts of Finland boats are still formed in this way. Sometimes the steam is created by filling the thoroughly dampened hull with hot stones; sometimes—as among the Alakalufs—the wet hull is banked all around with glowing coals. Once steam has softened the wood, the hull is stretched by hammering thwarts into position at right angles to its sides; they are left there to hold the hull in shape until the wood dries. As it dries it contracts, and the thwarts are held tight

by the shrinking process, to serve later as seating.

Dugouts have been known to reach a length of 60 feet, and some may have carried as many as 100 passengers and paddlers. In such boats men have covered great distances. The anthropologists studying the Alakalufs report that one of the tribe's dugouts was dispatched to meet a passenger at a steamship landing 160 miles away. But though they journey far, the Alakalufs hug the coast and prefer to portage across peninsulas rather than risk the breaking waves and treacherous currents swirling around the headlands.

The early Scandinavians must have been every bit as cautious. Crossing the fjords, they would have had to paddle against strong tides. And crossing channels and sounds they would have encountered swift, unpredictable currents. Yet, cross them they occasionally did—or so, at least, the evidence suggests. Flint implements of Danish design dating from at least 4000 B.C. have been found in western Sweden, directly across the turbulent Kattegat strait from the point in northern Jutland where the flint tools were made, a distance of some 40 miles. Although the ancient seafarers could have taken a roundabout and presumably safer route—island-hopping from Zealand to southern Sweden and moving up the Swedish coastline—the position of the two flint sites, exactly opposite each other, argues for the shorter, far more venturesome voyage.

Similar evidence points to a sea link between Norway and northern Jutland during the same period, either around the Kattegat strait or across almost 80 miles of open water. And by 3000 B.C. seafarers from southern Scandinavia apparently were voyaging along more than 600 miles of Sweden's east coast.

As far north as the Swedish province of Vaasterbotten, archaeologists have found caches of semifinished flint implements, one of the surest signs that the coast was visited by trading expeditions. The rough tools, later to be finished by their ultimate owners, were deposited in the caches for safekeeping—much as a modern merchant warehouses part of his stock.

Clearly these mariners were remarkable navigators. They guided their boats into unknown waters, sometimes out of sight of land, relying on little except instinct, supported by their knowledge of the migrating and feeding habits of fishes and birds. Several thousand years later the Vikings are supposed to have released ravens from their ships when out of sight of land and watched their flight to determine the direction of the shore. Perhaps their forebears did the same. The Vikings also knew that the sun rose and set in different quarters at different times of the year, and may have told time by the length of the shadow cast by the gunwales. The earlier Scandinavians, too, may have been equipped with such knowledge.

But there must have been times when familiar signs were obscured, when the seamen had to paddle for shore through driving rain or dense fog, relying solely on blind chance and the gods. And even when the weather was fine, the voyages must have been arduous. Since there was not enough room for the crew to rest by stretching out on the bottom of the boat, they must have put ashore every night to sleep. A lack of storage space must also have forced them to replenish their food and water supplies at regular, short intervals.

Why did they embark on such perilous odysseys? The answer is trade. Indeed, the commodities they carried and brought back provide the clearest evidence of the extent of the Northmen's travels during prehistoric times. At first, these journeys were probably nothing more than expeditions to the source of a particular tool material needed by the voyaging hunters themselves. Later, when men were able to collect more raw materials than they needed for their own immediate use, and began to exchange them, the journeys became genuine trading missions, the products of one region being bartered for those of another—flint for sealskin, for instance, or amber for antler, or sea salt for a basket of grain.

From earliest times flint was one of the prime trade items of the Scandinavian voyagers. An opaque silica substance found in chalk deposits, flint was the finest of all Stone Age tool materials—and Denmark and southern Sweden had flint in abundance. In many places it could be picked off the ground or pried from exposed outcroppings in the form of nodules. Furthermore, it was of the very highest quality: the nodules were large, and generally free of cracks and cavities, just right for making such heavy-duty tools as axes and adzes.

The peoples of southern Scandinavia were quick to exploit their good fortune. According to British archaeologist J. G. D. Clark, the flint deposits of the region "supported the most splendid flint industry in Europe". The industry was spawned by the growing population of Scandinavian farmers who needed more axes, more sickles, more weapons to protect their homesteads. So great did the farmers' demand for flint become that men in Denmark, as well as in other flint-producing regions, began to mine the substance from pits and underground tunnels. The best flint, in fact, lay beneath the earth's surface, where it was protected from weathering. Not until late in the

Stone Age, however, did men feel the need to go after this buried treasure. Then, using picks and wedges made from antlers, and shovels made of wood or the broad shoulder blades of cattle, they dug shafts into the earth as deep as 40 feet.

Most of the Scandinavian flint mines were concentrated in northern Jutland and in the southeastern part of the Danish islands of Zealand, Lolland and Moen. Archaeologists began investigating these prehistoric mines during the 1950s. Along with the pits and shafts themselves, they discovered some interesting facts about the mining operations. For instance, the miners were not always successful. Sometimes they dug for several weeks without uncovering a single vein of usable flint. When this happened, Danish archaeologist C. J. Becker has suggested, "strong language was used while the pit was being filled in again".

The archaeologists also discovered that the flint was rough-shaped right at the mine site—made into "blanks" that could be refined by toolmakers elsewhere. Around many of the mine openings, and in the pits of abandoned mines, investigators came upon quantities of flint flakes and half-completed tools, discarded because they were flawed. Thus, the traders, in effect, were carrying only saleable goods—flint that had been pre-tested for its grain and chipping quality. This conscientiousness must have greatly enhanced both their bartering position and the return on their investment. By carrying rough-shaped flints instead of raw nodules, the traders packed their boats with more merchandise as well as merchandise of proven quality.

The Northmen also trafficked among themselves in another tool material —greenstone, a hard volcanic rock. One prime source was a tiny island now called Hespriholmen, four miles off the southwestern coast of Norway. Lying roughly midway between Bergen and Stavanger in the archipelago that fringes Norway's long coastline, Hespriholmen is less than 300 yards long and only 100 yards wide—a mere dot among its sisters. Yet the island was visited regularly by fisherfolk who were contemporaneous with the late Fosna reindeer hunters, and it continued to be visited right up through the days of the first slash-and-burn farmers.

To get to the greenstone deposits on Hespriholmen these ancient Northmen not only had to paddle four miles out to sea, they also had to round the island and come in on its seaward side, where the quarry lay —but where the surf is almost always rough and choppy. Beaching their frail boats, the prospectors pried and hammered lumps of greenstone from the island's rocky face. When their boats were laden with the jagged cargo, they shoved off through the heaving surf and headed for home. It is difficult to imagine a more precarious quarrying operation. The quarries themselves are still there. Though once they were at sea level, they now form great cavities 20 feet up the side of the cliff—further evidence of how much Scandinavia has risen since the weight of the glacial ice ceased to depress the land.

In time, the quarrying at Hespriholmen became part of what must have been an extensive toolmaking industry. On the near-by, larger island of Boemlo archaeologists have come upon tremendous piles of greenstone flakes, as many as 1,700 flakes in a single square yard. Apparently Hespriholmen's greenstone was transported to Boemlo to be manufactured into tools. Whether the people who took it there were the same ones who carried away the finished product is not known. But the greenstone tools eventually reached the mainland; there they were widely distributed, probably as articles of trade, in settlements scattered all along the rivers and coasts of western and southern Norway.

If stone for tools was the seafaring Northmen's chief stock in trade, their most valuable cargo, by far, was amber (*pages 86-91*). The fossilized resin of ancient conifers, amber washed up on Baltic beaches, and was collected and cherished by the earliest Stone Age peoples living along the Baltic. They fashioned the sea-worn chunks into polished charms or ornaments that they wore or carried with them. The amber amulet of the Meiendorf hunter, the amber beads buried by the Barkaer farmer beneath his house —both were believed to be connected in some way with the spirit world. Perhaps amber, translucent and golden, represented the sun to the Northmen; perhaps it was thought to possess the sun's life-giving powers of light and warmth.

Around 2400 B.C. the peoples of Britain and Europe became aware of Baltic amber. Some of it reached them through channels of trade, and as the demand grew, the Nordic seafarers came to play an ever-increasing rôle in amber's distribution. From the west coast of Denmark there eventually flowed a golden river of amber, some of it going westwards across the North Sea to Britain and Ireland, but most of it moving southwards to Europe. Carried up the river Elbe by boats to central Germany, then loaded onto pack animals for the trip across the Brenner Pass into Italy, it was transferred at Adriatic ports to boats bound for Greece and the Aegean, perhaps even for the cities of Egypt—there to adorn the bosoms of fashionable ladies and to enrich the tombs of princes.

In return for their amber the Northmen received metal—gold, copper and tin. With the new impetus for increased trade provided by the introduction of metals and metalworking into Scandinavia late in the Third Millennium B.C., shipbuilding and seafaring flourished as never before. By 1500 B.C. the Northmen's vessels were venturing far beyond Scandinavian waters. They were regularly challenging the open sea to bring back gold from Ireland and copper and tin from Britain; a few experts think they may have ventured southwards along the coast of France and Spain to enter the Mediterranean and trade directly with the urban peoples living on Crete and in Greece, Egypt and the Middle East.

Along the Norwegian coast and up into central Sweden there are Bronze Age records on rock of what these seagoing ships looked like. Thousands of depictions of them are engraved on boulders, on cliffs, on bedrock scoured clean by the glaciers (*pages 69-73*). No longer are the boats simple dugouts or skin boats. Instead, they are high-prowed, broad-beamed craft with keels that project beyond the hulls fore and aft, and with carved posts at prow and stern. Occasionally the decorative prow resembles an animal head and, in fact, it may have been the actual skull of a horse or a cow instead of a carved replica. Sometimes the ships are shown with human figures aboard, indicated by vertical lines rising above the gunwales. And sometimes the figures are brandishing war clubs or battle-axes. The largest ship drawing is 15 feet long; the largest crew shown adds up to an extraordinary 81 men. From a few of the ships carved on the rocks rise vague shapes that may or may not represent some sort of sail.

A ship monument, 54 feet from bow to stern with a 13-foot beam, marks a Bronze Age grave on the Swedish island of Gotland. Many similar monuments have been discovered, and archaeologists think they represent vessels in which the dead journeyed across a great sea to the other world.

Until the present century, these cryptic rock drawings were almost the only clues to the boatbuilding techniques of Bronze Age Scandinavians. Tantalizing hints of the contours of the boats were glimpsed now and then in the shapes of graves—especially on the Baltic island of Gotland, where people presumably depended a great deal on the sea. The graves on the island are often outlined with a rim of stones whose shape is reminiscent of a high-prowed ship (*page 81*). Looking at such symbolic replicas, scholars could only guess how the real boats had been made. And many questions about them went unanswered. What materials had gone into them? Were they lashed together or pegged together? Were they rowed or paddled? How were they steered?

Today some of the questions have been answered because of a dramatic find made in 1921 in a Danish bog. Like so many similar discoveries, it was made inadvertently by a group of farmers cutting peat for their cooking stoves and hearth fires. The bog is called Hjortspring on the island of Als in southern Denmark, and the object unearthed is a plank-built boat—one of the oldest vessels ever found in Scandinavia (*pages 82-83*), and the best preserved. The boat has a double prow, and its ends are carved into long beaks, which extend well beyond the hull itself—just like the boats in the rock drawings. Its lines, however, are sleeker and it held a veritable arsenal of shields and weapons. Presumably this particular boat was a war canoe, designed for speed and manœuvrability.

Pollen analysis of the bog and the sophistication of the weapons found with the boat date the Hjortspring craft at about 350 B.C., near the beginning of the Scandinavian Iron Age. But its obvious resemblance to the earlier boats in the rock drawings suggests that both were built in essentially the same way. Also, the techniques used in its construction were so advanced that vessels of this type could scarcely have been an Iron Age invention. They must have evolved over many, many generations.

Measuring about 62 feet from stem to stern, the entire boat consists of only seven pieces of wood. The bottom is a single piece of linden, hollowed out dugout fashion—a technique that more than hints at how this type of boat came to be. On each side of the bottom are added two planks of linden, raising the height of the gunwales to a much more seaworthy 28 inches. The two remaining pieces are pre-cut bow and stern ends, tapered chunks that are lashed onto the main body of the boat fore and aft. All seven component parts have been whittled and carved and pierced to provide for various structural elements in a dazzling display of early Iron Age carpentry. The gunwale, for instance, was shaped to provide a handgrip by gouging away some of the wood beneath the edge. Cleats for positioning and fastening the ribs to the hull were carved into the four linden planks instead of being added on as separate elements. And the Hjortspring boat's curiously projecting beaks are sculpted from the bottom plank and from the chunks that form the boat's double prow. (The purpose of these curious beaks continues to be a mystery: they have been referred to as battering rams, stabilizers, handles with which to lift and carry the boat, artistic vestiges of the structural framework of Stone Age skin boats—all of which, part of which or none of which may be true.)

The planks of the Hjortspring boat were sewn and lashed together, perhaps with twisted animal gut (long since rotted away), in such fashion that the top

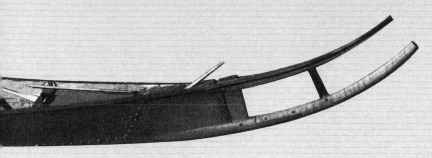

A Danish reconstruction of a 2,000-year-old war canoe dug up in a peat bog at Hjortspring, Denmark, closely resembles ancient boats pictured in Scandinavian rock carvings. The original, 62 feet long, apparently was seized in battle and sacrificed. It held a cargo of wooden shields (below), iron weapons and coats of chain mail.

plank overlapped the one beneath it. The Iron Age builder perforated the planks at intervals to receive the cording and then, like any modern boat owner, caulked the seams and construction holes with resin. Today this kind of boat, with overlapping planks, is said to be clinker-built, or clincher-built. The technique was used elsewhere in ancient times, notably on the Ganges in India; but in Europe the clinker-built boat was typically Scandinavian. Other European hulls tended to be made by butting the planks together edge to edge in a method known as carvel-built—a name derived from the light sailing-ships that used the technique: the caravels that plied the relatively gentle waters of the Mediterranean. Clinker construction has one distinct advantage: it produces a more flexible hull, one better able to withstand the buffeting of a heavy sea.

Because no provision was made for oarlocks on the gunwales of the Hjortspring boat, experts conclude that it was driven by paddles. And indeed, the position of the thwarts reinforces this conclusion: they are angled. Thus, the shoulders of the crew —who used the thwarts for seats—would be thrust outwards over the gunwales in the best position for producing strong, powerful paddle strokes. At the same time, though the boat contains no locks for oars, it probably once had two locks for a steering paddle —one at each end of the boat. Probably the helmsman simply moved from one end of the boat to the other when he wanted to change its direction. In operating his steering oar the helmsman may have faced the *stjornbordi*, or steering side of the boat, with his back to the *bakbordi*, terms used by later Northmen to designate starboard and port. (The English word starboard derives from the Norse *stornbordi*, though *bakbordi* has no such linguistic connection with port.)

So well designed and skilfully made were these early boats that Scandinavians continued to use the same building methods right up through Viking times. The double ends, the overlapping planks, the practice of sewing and lashing together the various parts —all these features appeared on the Vikings' dragon boats at the end of the First Millennium A.D., when Northmen were considered the best shipbuilders and the most audacious seafarers in Europe. Indeed, many of these ancient techniques are still employed today. Double-ended, clinker-built fishing dories can still be seen pulled up on beaches and tidal flats not only in Scandinavia but in every country of Europe and the New World where Nordic shipwrights once plied their trade and passed on their secrets.

But what of the mystery of the Hjortspring boat? What was it doing in a Danish bog? Who put it there?

And why? No one knows for sure, but archaeologists are willing to make some educated guesses. The bog was once a lake and, like so many ancient Scandinavian lakes, it may have been regarded as sacred. At the time the boat was sunk, all of northern Europe was wracked by the squabbles of warring tribes: a growing population and a shift in climate from warm to cool set man against man in the struggle for food and living space. The Hjortspring boat may have been seized as booty in a clash between two tribes over just such an issue. In gratitude to the gods for the favorable outcome of the battle, amid much celebration, the victors presumably hoisted the warship on their shoulders and bore it through the woods to the sacred lake. There they filled it with the captured weapons and sank it—an offering of thanks for which scholars living thousands of years later have their own reasons for being thankful.

The Gold of the North— Amber

Amber has been cherished for ornamental use since the early Stone Age, making it, along with wood, rock and bone, one of man's oldest artistic mediums. A petrified resin, it is soft enough to work without the use of special tools, does not break when carved and can be drilled and polished easily. These qualities, along with its ready availability throughout much of northern Europe, where it washed up on Baltic beaches, its pleasant fragrance and smooth texture and its glowing beauty, made it attractive to prehistoric Scandinavian craftsmen. Moreover, it seemed endowed with magical characteristics. Weight for size, it was strangely light, and when rubbed, it built up a charge of static electricity (The Greek word for amber is *elektron*.) Its reputation spread south, and Greeks and Romans took to wearing amber necklaces as charms, convinced that amber helped cure such complaints as rheumatism, toothaches and throat infections.

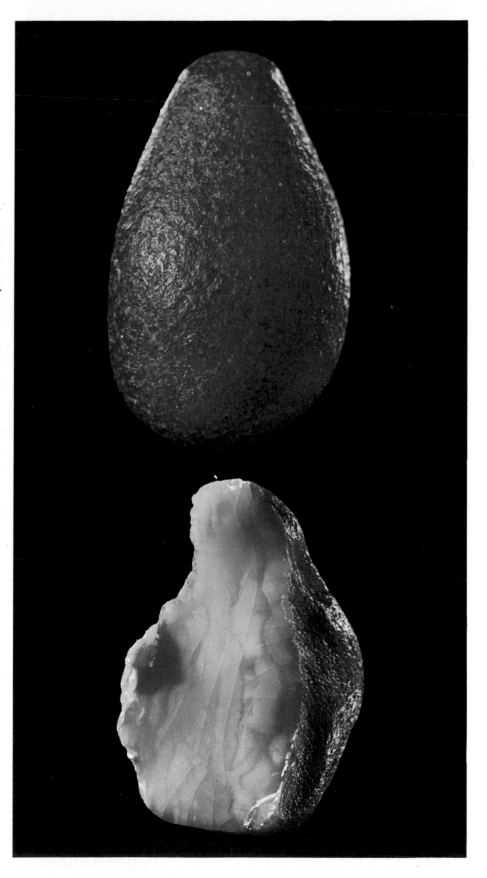

Preserving the perfect shape formed while clinging to a coniferous tree 70 or 80 million years ago, a rare drop of raw amber (top)—enlarged almost four times—is crusted with age. A similar piece (bottom), after being cracked open, reveals the typical golden colour and the glassy texture of fine amber.

Fossilized Sunshine in its Varied Forms

Though all amber originates in the same way—as fossilized sap from a conifer—time and the elements create many different varieties. Most amber ranges from pale yellow (*numbers 6 and 7*) to deep brown (*2 and 4*). But thousands of years of weathering have given some chunks a reddish hue (*1*), and impurities have made others dark (*3 and 5*). Samples within the same colour range vary depending on whether the piece is clear or cloudy (*10*) or has interior fracture marks. Sometimes a clear sample (*8*) will be laced with a slight opacity called *Flohm*—a German word meaning goose fat. Additional variations in amber reflect its milieu: amber washed ashore from the sea, for example, will have a thin orange crust (*9*), while amber taken from the earth will have a thicker brown crust (*2*).

Each piece of amber—as indicated by this array of samples—has its own personality, determined by its colour and clarity and even by imprisoned impurities. Wood dust (3 and 5) is common, but a more spectacular example (11) is the 60-million-year-old insect—looking much like one of its descendants of today—preserved intact in a small slab of Baltic amber.

87

Beauty Enhanced by Magic

Although they lacked readily available supplies of gold, silver, copper and tin for use in jewellery, prehistoric Scandinavian artisans were compensated by having at least one plentiful, precious resource of their own in the form of amber. From the beginning, they seem to have viewed it as exceptional. The earliest reindeer hunters used amber for amulets (*page 34*), while later Northmen strung it on necklaces (*right*) or sculpted it into naturalistic animal forms (*far right*). Seeming to catch and hold the light of the sun, amber became associated with sun worship, as gold was in other parts of the world. Its supposed magical qualities, in addition to its beauty, enhanced its value and desirability. Indeed, amber came to be so admired throughout Europe that in Rome, for example, a small amber statue cost more than several slaves.

These strings of amber (right), dating from the Stone Age, may have been worn for protection by Scandinavian women and their children; the amber horse of the Second Millennium B.C. *(far right) —reproduced slightly larger than its actual size—apparently also served to safeguard its owner from evil forces.*

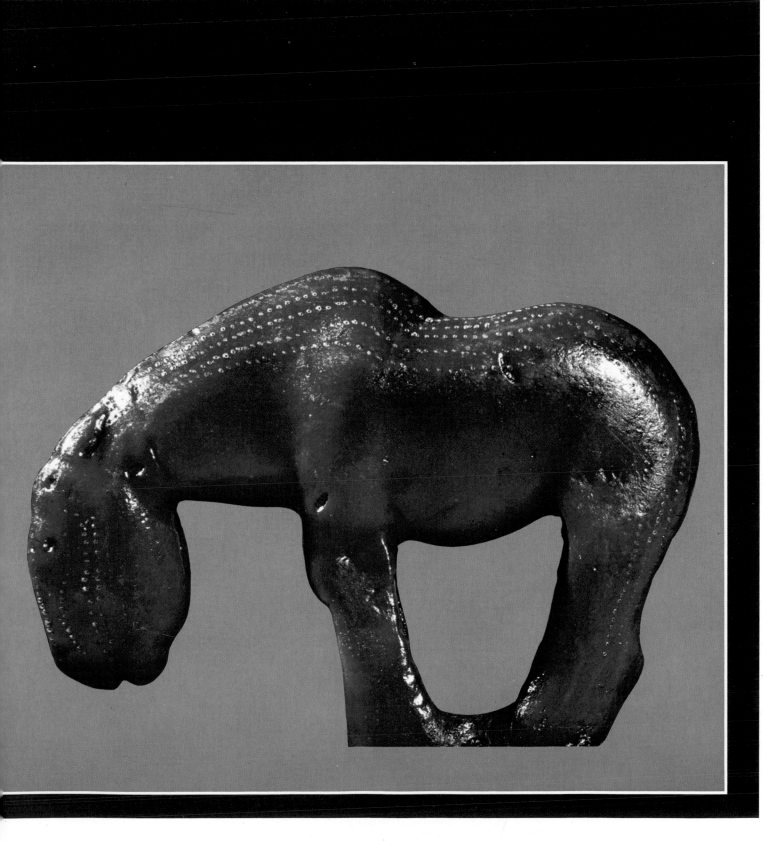

In the Hands of Classical Artists

Around 2000 B.C. the Northmen began to come into direct contact with people from southern Europe. It was not long before the southerners became enchanted by the decorative potential of amber and the Northmen, in turn, by the uses of metal, to which they were newly exposed.

Amber, as an exchange medium for metal, thus started flowing south over an elaborate network of trade routes developed during the Scandinavian Bronze Age. Southern craftsmen soon were carving northern amber into a wide range of fantastic shapes for their wealthy customers. It became the rage of the upper classes first in Greece, then in Rome. Greek legend had it that amber was the hardened tears of the sisters of Phaethon, a youth struck down by Zeus for driving the Sun God's chariot.

Amber, in the hands of southern craftsmen in the centuries immediately before and after Christ, took forms as diverse as these: a jar adorned with cupids (1), a lid in the shape of a satyr (2), a woman standing behind a man (3), a carving of a satyr (4), a clasp with bands of gold and amber (5) and a bird (6). Each is less than five inches long.

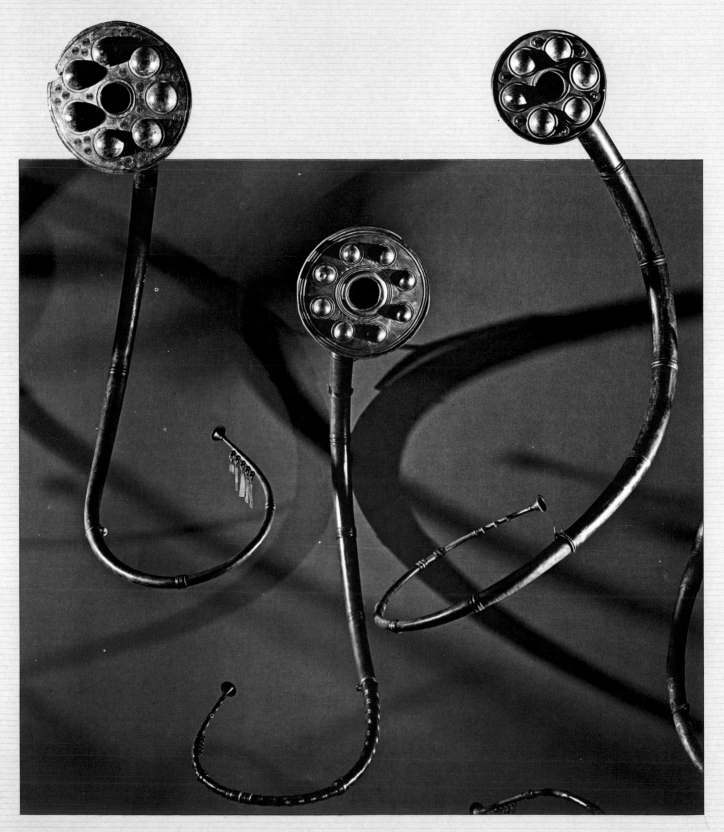

Looking back to the Bronze Age, modern Scandinavians come literally face to face with their ancestors. There are, for example, the remains of the young woman of Egtved in eastern Jutland (*page 99*). Lithe, fair-haired and barely 20, she was placed more than 3,000 years ago in a coffin hollowed from an oak log. Her blonde hair falls over her face, her fingernails are carefully trimmed. She wears a jacket of brown wool with elbow-length sleeves and a short skirt of loose woollen cords that ends well above her knees. Tied to her belt are a comb and a small, spiked bronze disc engraved with a spiral design; on her wrists she wears two bronze bracelets. A soft blanket of cowhide envelops her; and just before the lid was closed, someone dropped a sprig of flowering yarrow into the coffin, a gift of the season—summer-time.

There is also the young woman of Skrydstrup, just a little to the south of Egtved. She is ash-blonde, tall and slender, with a narrow face and elegant, long eyelashes. On her head she wears an open-work cap of woven horsehair, on her feet simple leather moccasins. In each ear she wears a ring of pure gold. Her jacket is of wool and so is the long skirt that reaches her ankles and resembles nothing so much as the homespun garb worn by medieval peasant women. But the young woman of Skrydstrup—like the Egtved girl—was no poor peasant. Her coffin was enclosed in an enormous mound of earth, 40 feet in diameter

Sinuous musical instruments called lurs attest to the skills of Scandinavian Bronze Age smiths. Measuring about four feet long and made up of individually cast bronze sections joined by rings, the lurs come apart for ease of carrying. Since many of these mournful-sounding instruments—usually found in pairs—have been uncovered in sacrificial bogs, archaeologists believe they were played during rituals and then sacrificed.

and five feet high, befitting a personage of rank.

There are other bodies, too. From various Bronze Age burial sites in Denmark have come the remains of an old man, fair-haired and clean-shaven, wearing a woollen cloak and tunic, and a high woollen hat; a young man wrapped in a cloak and shod in leather moccasins, with a bronze sword lying across his breast; an older woman, perhaps 50 or 60, with a bronze collar encircling her neck, bronze ornaments on her skirt, and a bronze dagger, comb and spiked disc suspended from her belt. None of these three people are so well preserved as the two young women of Egtved and Skrydstrup, but, with others like them, all give life to a period of Scandinavian prehistory as no mere artifacts can.

These were the people who launched Scandinavia into a golden age. It was they who, along with their wealthy contemporaries, commissioned the glittering ornaments of bronze and gold, who wielded the bronze swords, axes and daggers that are found in such abundance all over the Northlands. And it is they for whom the landscape of southern Scandinavia is everywhere breasted with massive burial mounds. But how is it that the remains of some of them have survived when so many later generations have vanished without a trace? The answer lies in the way they were buried: in oak coffins resting on beds of hard subsoil surrounded by damp earth.

Under normal circumstances everything in a grave will rot sooner or later from the interaction of bacteria, rain-water and air filtering down through the soil. Metal will oxidize, and the body, the clothes and the coffin will decompose. But if the coffin is placed on hardpan or clay, or even on compacted layers of heather, the water flow is checked; the soil around the coffin becomes saturated, and water fills the coffin itself; chemicals leach out of the soil into the coffin, and oxygen and bacteria are excluded. This is what happened in a few of the Scandinavian Bronze Age burial mounds. At the same time, the water-logged oak coffins released their tannic acid so that the bodies inside were, quite literally, tanned—just as leather is sometimes tanned by being buried in the earth along with chips of oak bark. In fact, Shakespeare's grave digger in *Hamlet* had some knowledge of this phenomenon.

"How long will a man lie i' the earth ere he rot?" asks the melancholy Prince of Denmark.

"Faith," replies the grave digger, "If he be not rotten before he die . . . he will last you some eight year or nine year; a tanner will last you nine year."

"Why he more than another?"

"Why, sir, his hide is so tanned with his trade that he will keep out water a great while, and your water is a sore decayer of your whoreson dead body."

Aided by the silent testimony of the oak coffin, it is possible to piece together the intimate details of life and death in an age long gone. But in order to tell the full story of that age it is necessary to go back some 900 years before the Egtved girl was even born —back to about 2400 B.C.

Some 4,300 years ago the Northmen had not yet learned the art of metalworking, though a few Bell Beaker People, Europe's itinerant tinkers, had apparently come to Scandinavia and left local inhabitants spellbound with their ability to melt and transform a hard, glittering substance few, if any, had seen before —copper. Along with these tinkers, another group of people probably began to make their presence felt

A mysterious bronze object, discovered in southern Sweden, consists of a 16-inch plate resting on an openwork base cast in 10 pieces. Connected in some way with sun worship, it has been interpreted by some puzzled experts as an altar, by others as a sacred drum. All that is certain is that it came from central Europe; a similar one has turned up in Hungary.

among the farmers, hunters and fishermen of the Northlands. Bands of nomadic stockbreeders from far to the east apparently pushed into Jutland and the Danish islands during the same period. Brandishing the battle-axes that became their trademark, these aggressive wanderers could take whatever land they wanted and make it their own.

The Battle-Axe People were but a few of the great numbers of tribesmen who had been pouring out of the arid wastelands of central Russia for generations, searching for better pastures for their horses, cattle, sheep and goats. Accompanied by livestock, they made their way into western Europe; some turned south into Greece and Macedonia, while others cut a broad swath across Germany into Scandinavia.

Wherever they went, these tribesmen had one enormous advantage: the horse. Though apparently they had not yet learned how to ride the animal, they used it—and oxen as well—to pull vehicles, thus achieving unprecedented mobility. Hitched to wagons, the beasts enabled them to transport their families and household effects over great distances.

Everywhere the progress of these tribesmen is marked by the graves in which they buried their dead. They did not use the stone graves of the dolmen and passage-grave builders, but low earthen mounds meant to contain one body—though in time the mounds grew quite high and wide, as succeeding generations buried their own dead on top of them. The bodies were always buried lying on one side, facing south—a practice probably carried from the Russian steppes. A male corpse was invariably accompanied by a prized battle-axe made of smooth-polished stone. By a curious cultural inversion, this axe was a copy of a copper type the invaders had used back home on the steppes; it even mimicked the raised ridge of a casting seam.

The invasion of Europe by nomadic herders did not take place in an organized assault, but rather over the course of many generations. Nor does the invasion seem to have been a particularly violent one. Attacks there may have been, with homesteads and villages put to flames. Often as not, though, the newcomers apparently settled down peacefully beside the native population and took possession of the marginal lands outside the cultivated areas, where the soil was too poor for crop raising but rich enough to provide good grazing for large herds of cattle, sheep and goats. The newcomers' effect on the farmers was gradual but pervasive—extending perhaps even to language. Since the people from the steppes are believed to have spoken an Indo-European tongue, it may have been through them that some modern European languages, including the Germanic tongues of Scandinavia, took rudimentary form.

But their cultural influence, however strong, was by no means one-sided: in the Northlands, for instance, the Battle-Axe People who arrived around the middle of the Third Millennium B.C. ultimately were as much marked by the local people as the local people were marked by them. In time the newcomers adopted the axes, daggers, spears and arrows used by the resident farmers. They even began to practise some farming along with their stockbreeding. Also like the farmers, they fell under the influence of metalworkers from the south, so that by 2000 B.C. Battle-Axe graves began to contain copper axes and daggers, and spiralling copper arm bands.

Thus, little by little the cultural differences among the various peoples dwelling in southern Scandinavia

disappeared. Farmers, hunters, fishermen, herders, craftsmen and traders adopted one another's ways of doing things, married their children to one another's children. By early in the Second Millennium B.C. customs, tools, weapons, pottery and burial practices had become practically indistinguishable.

During this period of merging and mingling, in the centuries immediately after 2000 B.C., the Northmen took the first steps in the production of bronze. Several centuries later they ranked among the finest bronzesmiths in Europe—despite the fact that Scandinavia lacked readily available supplies of copper and tin, the two metals from which bronze is made.

The first bronze to enter Scandinavia apparently came from the copper and tin regions of Britain and central Europe. Very likely much of it arrived in the packs of itinerant smiths who had left those regions to seek markets elsewhere. Once settled in Scandinavia, the smiths undoubtedly relied more upon the rich metal resources of central Europe for their raw material: from the mines of Germany, Austria, Hungary and Czechoslovakia traders carried the metals north, along the river Elbe.

The Northmen probably learned from British and other European smiths how to smelt copper and tin, how to mix them in the right proportions, how to fashion stone and clay moulds into which the molten metal could be poured. And because foreigners were the Northmen's first teachers, it is not surprising that

A gold-plated disc, 10 inches in diameter, rests in a bronze chariot drawn by a bronze horse. Dating from 1000 B.C., this relic was ploughed up in 1902 in Denmark's Trundholm bog by a farmer who gave it to his daughter as a plaything. The sun chariot, now in the National Museum, probably embodies the belief that a horse pulled the sun through the heavens.

many of the first Scandinavian bronzes were little more than crude copies of British and European models. But the skills of the Northmen grew, and eventually Scandinavian smiths were using the technique of lost-wax casting to produce sophisticated objects of their own. (In lost-wax casting a wax model is made, then covered with clay and heated so that the wax runs out, leaving only the clay mould into which the molten metal is poured.)

By 1500 B.C. the Northmen had outstripped their teachers in the skill and delicacy with which they turned raw metal into finished products. All through southern Scandinavia—in Denmark, Sweden and Norway—archaeologists have unearthed the bronze hoards of native smiths, buried for safe-keeping and never reclaimed, as well as traces of work sites. Moulds of every kind, half-finished castings, crucibles of clay and stone, anvils, hammers, chisels, punches, awls and knives attest to the versatility of these craftsmen. At the site of one Bronze Age village near Stockholm, archaeologists uncovered so many signs of metalworking that it seems a good part of the village must have been engaged in bronze production.

But while fine bronzework was greatly admired, it was still rare and expensive. So to satisfy some customers, knappers went to the trouble—as had the earlier Battle-Axe People—of producing stone objects that were close copies of bronze prototypes. On the Danish island of Funen, for instance, a flint dagger has come to light that is a replica of a bronze design, right down to the fish-tail pommel. But sometimes the knappers carried their artistry almost too far. Also found at Funen was a flint copy of a curved bronze slashing sword. Used for anything but ceremony or show, such a weapon would shatter at one stroke.

The range of bronze goods produced by ancient Scandinavian craftsmen is remarkable. Along with axes, swords and daggers, a wealth of intricately fashioned objects has been uncovered: pins, neck rings, razors, tweezers and, most astonishing of all, musical instruments. The magnificent ceremonial horns known as lurs are like no other bronze artifacts found anywhere else in Europe. These graceful musical instruments are never less than three feet long, and some measure five feet. They were cast in sections and joined to make a beautiful double-swung curve; apparently they were always made in matching pairs, curved in opposite directions like the horns of a bull. Experts assume that lurs were always played in pairs as well. They could produce, as experiments have demonstrated, a full register of notes, and modern Scandinavian composers have even employed the lurs in orchestral pieces—though, as one prehistorian felt compelled to point out, "without great success".

Most such metalwork was done in southern Scandinavia. Bronze objects turn up only rarely in more northerly regions, and those that do appear were presumably carried there by traders; the area remained relatively untouched by influences from the rest of Europe. Since Scandinavians near the Arctic Circle were so remote from the source of metals, and because the harsh climate and rugged terrain were hardly conducive to farming or herding, they continued to live like Stone Age hunters and fishermen.

Denmark was the real centre of Scandinavia's bronze industry and the hub of its Bronze Age culture —partly because Denmark lay closest to the sources of ore, and partly because the Danes' amber-rich coasts provided a ready and seemingly inexhaust-

Text continued on page 103

Treasures Sealed For ever in Coffins of Oak

Dotting the fertile countryside of Denmark are more than 300 man-made hillocks covering the remains of Bronze Age men and women. In a few rare instances, water has combined with chemicals in the soil to help preserve not only the oak coffins and the bodies in them but even clothing. The contents of the women's graves offer an eerie glimpse of the fashions and luxuries of 1500 B.C. On the following pages are pictures of garments and treasures found buried with the Egtved girl (*below*) and with other prehistoric Danish women. The quality of their possessions as well as the elaborate way in which they were interred suggest that they were not commoners, but highly regarded members of the community.

This 3,500-year-old oak coffin, found in 1921 in Egtved, Jutland, contains the clothing, ornaments and blonde hair of a young woman. Buried with her were the cremated bones of a seven-year-old child, perhaps offered as a sacrifice.

What Wealthy Women Wore

Wealthy Bronze Age women were buried with belongings appropriate to their station, including well-made jewellery and even weapons, like the bronze dagger at right. Some wore finely woven woollen clothes, remarkable to modern eyes particularly for the brevity of the cord skirts (far right). When dressed thus in life, they also donned—perhaps from a sense of propriety or as a warning to aggressive males—belt discs (below). These small, pointed shields dangled at their waists.

A spiral design decorates this belt disc (below) and part of an armband (right).

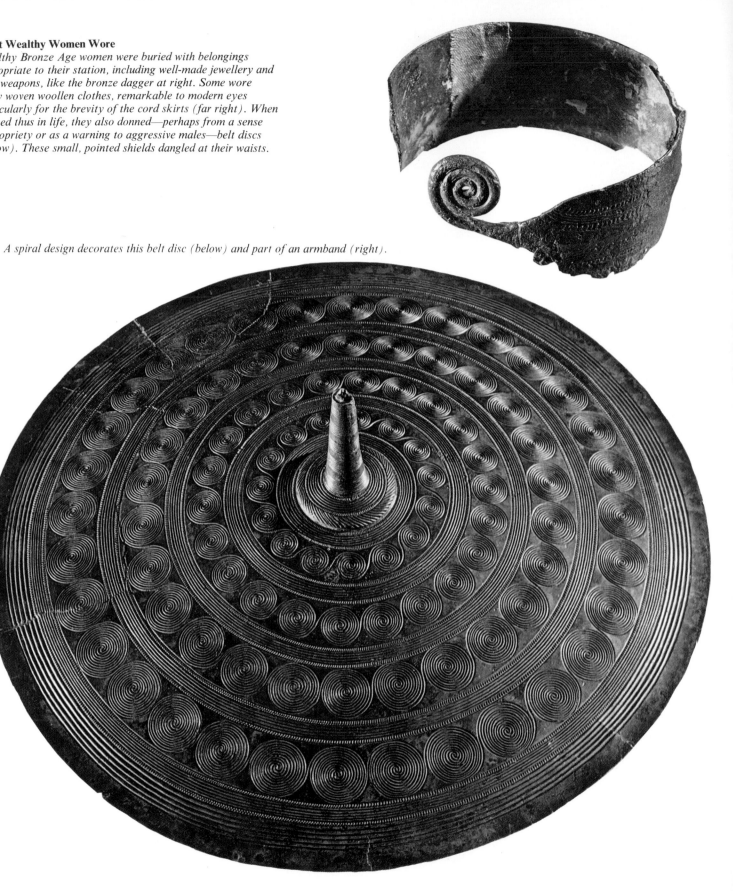

This double-edged bronze dagger is a small replica of a man's sword. Well-to-do women carried such daggers in their belts as signs of rank—and as protection against possible attack.

The jacket, belt and skirt of the Egtved girl (page 99) represent the height of Bronze Age fashion. The wool jacket is one piece, stitched at the side, with a hole cut for the neck and head. The more complicated mini-skirt is made from one continuous strand of twisted wool, looped up and down and tied at both top and bottom to hold it together.

ible supply of wealth to trade for copper and tin.

Usually the first of the Scandinavian lands to be influenced by new cultures from the south, Denmark became a conduit for many of the goods moving into and out of the Northlands. From here, amber and furs were carried by water and by overland trade routes to other parts of Europe, while copper, tin, bronze and gold in the form of ingots or finished articles in the latest styles moved northwards into the Scandinavian peninsula.

The Danes through whose hands passed the traffic in metals, furs and amber grew immensely rich and powerful. No doubt the richest of them built for themselves and their loved ones the great burial mounds from which the oak coffins have come. But the trade must also have benefited ordinary people: the metalsmiths and the farmers who did double-duty as shipwrights and amber gatherers.

Even the poorest farmers must have shared to some degree in the general affluence, though they probably derived more immediate profit from the warm and sunny climate that descended on southern Scandinavia during the Bronze Age, with temperatures warmer than today's. Under this beneficence of nature their fields yielded fine harvests of grain and other foodstuffs, and earning a living from the land must have been easier than it had ever been before.

At the heart of Denmark's new wealth were the harbours and trading stations located up and down Jutland's west coast and on the islands. Unfortunately, no complete coastal settlement has so far been discovered—some such sites now lie underwater—so any description of the activities that went on in them 3,500 years ago must be pieced together from finds made at various sites, bogs and tombs.

It is a sunny summer day around 1400 B.C. At one Danish trading centre, on the west coast of Jutland, a double-prowed long-boat manned by a score of tanned paddlers with sun-bleached hair has just returned from a voyage to the mouth of the Elbe. Outward bound they had taken amber and the pelts of foxes, seals, martens and bears brought to Jutland from Sweden, Norway and Finland. Heavier and richer than pelts taken in warmer climates, northern furs were much prized in central Europe. Now, on their homeward journey, the seamen carry ingots of copper, tin or bronze.

The seamen's home port is unimposing—little more than a collection of rectangular, mud-plastered houses with thatched roofs. But on this day the quiet beach has suddenly become an impromptu marketplace full of bustle and chatter. Village folk and traders from inland have come down to welcome the crew, to evaluate the size and worth of the cargo, and to bargain for the metals and whatever exotic trinkets the boatmen may have picked up abroad. At the edge of the crowd a string of pack horses and ox-carts is waiting to be loaded for the journey inland. The crowd is laughing, shouting, haranguing; everyone is trying to get the best bargain.

A market is always a good place to observe people in all their variety. Here, amid the clamour and the mingled smells of salt air and sweating bodies, a stranger can draw some generalizations about the local population. The first thing to be noticed is that many are fair-haired. Nearly everyone is dressed in garments woven of a coarse native wool, shading from brown to black. The men are well groomed, with clean-shaven cheeks and short hair. Typically, they wear knee-length tunics, fastened at one shoulder by two straps and drawn in at the waist with a belt of woven cording or leather. On damp or cool days, they don long, oval-shaped cloaks, folded at the neck to form a kind of shawl collar. Their usual head-gear is a round felt cap, and on their feet they have leather sandals, tied around the ankle with thongs. Sometimes, for warmth, cloth stockings are added.

The women too are dressed in wool, but their garments are more varied, and so are their hair styles. Some wear their hair cropped short, page-boy style; some allow their hair to grow long and pile it on top of their heads in elaborate arrangements held in place by net caps. Many of the women wear wide-necked shirts with three-quarter-length sleeves; sometimes the shirts are embroidered in wool of different shades, creating patterned designs. The skirts are either ankle length, gathered and looped over a belt at the waist, or very short.

Found nowhere else in the world, and at no other time in Scandinavia except during the warm, sunny centuries of the Bronze Age, the short, skimpy skirt is worn low on the hips and ends at mid-thigh (*page 101*). In fact, it is little more than a length of wool fringe, held together top and bottom by cording and wrapped twice around the body. Between the top of the skirt and the bottom of the tunic there is nothing but pale skin.

Some of the wealthier women modify this provocative garb by adding to their belts a bronze disc, nearly six inches in diameter, from which protrudes a spike. (This daunting object has been described by one student of prehistory as "an expression of the upper-class woman's absolute inviolability. Where she advances, gleaming with metal, men of lower birth must relinquish all playful fancies".)

Surveying the crowd in the busy market-place, an onlooker might notice another curious feature of the people's dress. Though all clothing, men's and women's alike, is of wool, some of it looks as though it were actually made of animal skins. The looped pile has the appearance and feel of fur, and the men's tunics and cloaks are made from expanses of cloth whose dimensions and shape closely resemble those of, say, deer hide; the long straps passing over one shoulder resemble the legs of a pelt. Even the manner in which the seams are joined is similar to that used in sewing leather: overlapped instead of turned under. It seems safe to conclude that, though the climate has warmed and times have changed, furs and hides still have a certain prestige value, and summer woollens are modelled after them.

Another thing the perceptive onlooker might notice is the ease with which one can tell the well-to-do from ordinary folk. Though the clothing of all is essentially the same in cut and texture, the rich are adorned with bronze and gold ornaments that poorer people cannot afford. They fasten their cloaks at the shoulder with bronze pins and brooches, and their costumes include bronze daggers and swords. Some even sport bronze shields, and one man wears a splendid bronze helmet with upward-curving horns. (The notion that the Vikings of several centuries later wore such horned helmets is a misconception; they wore conical iron headgear.)

Although all this military raiment suggests warfare, it may in fact have another purpose. If the onlooker were to draw close, he would discover that the swords show few signs of use, and in any case would seem to be too fragile and too cumbersome to serve their owners well in combat. The weapons are

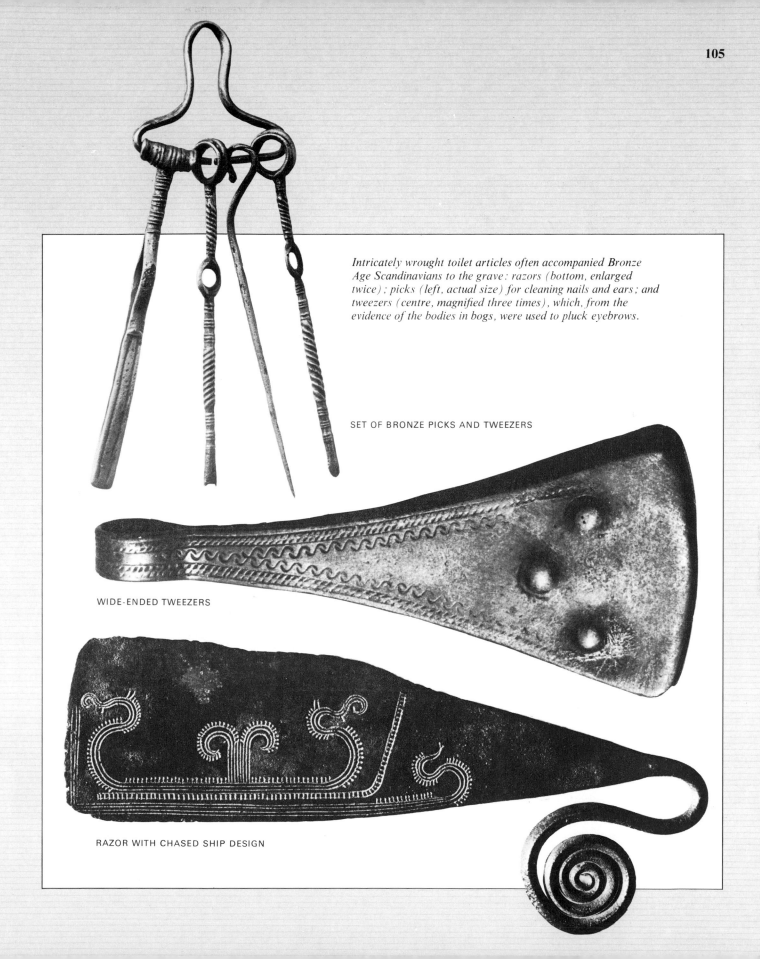

Intricately wrought toilet articles often accompanied Bronze Age Scandinavians to the grave: razors (bottom, enlarged twice); picks (left, actual size) for cleaning nails and ears; and tweezers (centre, magnified three times), which, from the evidence of the bodies in bogs, were used to pluck eyebrows.

SET OF BRONZE PICKS AND TWEEZERS

WIDE-ENDED TWEEZERS

RAZOR WITH CHASED SHIP DESIGN

probably worn as much for decoration as for defence.

The women are similarly bedecked. In addition to the belt disc with its intimidating spike, they too carry a bronze dagger. Perhaps the weapon, like the sword carried by the men, is a sign of rank, though doubtless it also served for cutting cloth and food. Of a decidedly more feminine character are the earrings, necklaces and pendants of gold—simple in design and starkly beautiful.

Gradually, as the beginning comes to an end, the impromptu market-place empties. The caravans pull out; the newly arrived boatmen go off to cavort or to sleep; and another trading ship, laden with furs and amber, departs. The people wander back to their homes, their workshops and their fields to resume their day-to-day activities.

Near one of the houses a smith, his fire burning, prepares to mix his newly acquired copper and tin. As he measures the metals, he turns over in his mind various ideas for incorporating into his standard repertoire some new design he has just seen in the imported wares at the market.

Were there time to explore the village itself and meet all its inhabitants, the visitor would find the work of the potters far less inspired than that done by the bronzesmith. Though well made and even graceful, the pots are devoid of ornamentation: unlike the creations of the late Stone Age, which were often lavishly decorated, they give the appearance of being strictly utilitarian. Perhaps the potters have been put off by the brilliant bowls and cups being produced by the smiths of the day—craftsmanship with which they do not hope to compete. More likely, there is less demand for their wares now that wooden bowls, carved with bronze tools, have come into in-

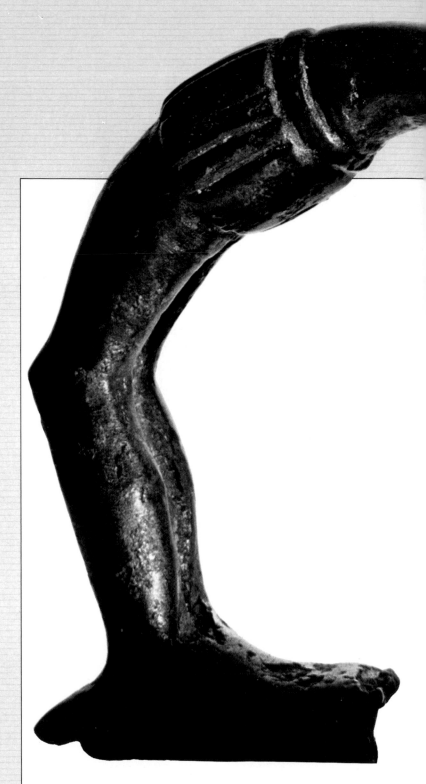

Her slim figure arched gracefully backwards, this two-inch bronze acrobatic dancer wears only a head-dress, a neck ring and the short, cord skirt typical of the Danish Bronze Age.

creasing use; such bowls wear better and break less readily than those made of fired clay. Possibly the best of the potters—or members of their families—have become smiths, for potters have a knowledge of pyrotechnics, gained through long years of working with kilns, that could give them an edge in mastering the techniques of smelting.

Generations of skill certainly have gone into the development of another major craft practised throughout the village—weaving. At least as far back as Maglemose times, men knew how to plait fishing traps and nets from grasses, strips of bark or strands of animal skins; even the walls of their shelters were woven of flexible tree boughs. Slowly such knowledge has been added to, and influences from abroad—from as far south as Greece—have crept in.

Still, the methods of these villagers are not sophisticated. During the previous autumn, when some of the sheep were slaughtered for food, the weavers collected wool by yanking the short summer fleece from the skins. In late spring, when the flocks were molting and their wool was at its best—long, thick and oily from the winter's growth—the weavers again collected fleece from their herds. Thus, by mixing thick wool and thin, light wool and dark, the weavers can vary the texture and colour of their finished cloth. And where the lanolin content is high, the wool is water resistant as well as warm.

In every hut there is a loom, and almost every female in the family carries a distaff and spindle with her wherever she goes, so that whenever her hands are free she can keep busy spinning wool into yarn. Her distaff is a stick on which the combed yarn is wound; it can be held in one hand or tucked under her arm. Her spindle is another stick with a hook at

Though cast in the late Bronze Age, two ribbed, bronze spearheads retain the shape and the simple but deadly contours of more primitive flint points.

An Armoury in Bronze

The introduction of bronze into Scandinavia around 1800 B.C., displacing flint as the basic weapon material, caused a revolution in armaments. Bronze had obvious advantages over stone. For one thing it could be made into a deadly military tool new to the north: the sword. But bronze had its drawbacks as well. Although strong it was brittle, and swords cast from the metal could be used effectively only as thrusting weapons; warriors who tried to slash with them risked having them break during combat.

Nevertheless, bronze swords were much in demand, and bronzesmiths lavished care on their manufacture. Intricate hilts were often cast with the blades as one piece, and many handles were inset with a range of decorative materials (*bottom right*). Interestingly, few of the swords recovered from graves and bogs show battle scars, leading archaeologists to believe that they probably had a dress function, symbolizing rank or authority, as well as a military function.

The more useful weapon of the period was almost certainly the bronze battle-axe. In the course of its development, the head of the battle-axe became smaller (top right, resting in its casting mould) and was attached to an angular handle at the end of a short wooden arm. The result was a light, well-balanced weapon with a lethal striking power.

In time bronze weapons became increasingly elaborate and unwieldy, until the introduction of iron-smelting rendered them—and bronze itself—as obsolete as bronze had made flint a thousand years earlier.

The head of a bronze battle-axe, only three and a half inches long, lies in the soap-stone mould in which it was cast. The axe and mould were found 10 miles apart in two separate Danish bogs.

These elaborate bronze sword hilts had decorative insets of bone, wood or a translucent substance made of amber boiled in oil, applied to the handles while still soft and allowed to harden.

one end and a weight, or whorl, attached to the other end. As she guides lengths of raw wool under the hook and onto the spindle, she sets the spindle twirling with her thumb and forefinger, and lets it drop, pulling a length of yarn with it. Kept in motion by its weight, the twirling spindle twists the wool into yarn and wraps the yarn into a ball.

When the spindle is full, the ball is removed and the whole process is begun all over again. The task is ceaseless and automatic, and by the time a girl is 10 or 12 years old, spinning is second nature to her: the distaff and spindle are such an intrinsic part of a woman's life that they often are buried with her.

When enough yarn is spun, the weaver threads her loom, a simple affair consisting of a wooden frame leaning against a wall of the hut (*page 29*). Vertical lengths of yarn, or warp, are suspended from the top of the frame and held taut at the bottom by a row of loom weights. Horizontal yarn, or woof, is guided in and out through the warp yarns, perhaps with the help of some sort of shuttle.

It seems that the village weavers have a simple version of the heddle—a length of wood designed to raise first one set of warp yarns then another, so that the shuttle can be pressed through them more easily. (Shuttles and heddles are pure surmise, but they would certainly explain the weavers' ability to turn out the quantities of cloth and the variety of weaves contained in the blankets, footcloths, cloaks, belts, tunics and skirts found in Bronze Age graves.)

Beyond the village lie the fields and pastures that supply the inhabitants with food. Though farmers are still in the majority the time is past when—as at Barkaer—everyone had to contribute to the settlement's food production. A better climate and better farming techniques now make it possible for fewer men to provide enough food for the growing population, some of whom, like the craftsmen, do no farming at all. In addition to wheat and barley, the villagers are able to raise—thanks to the warmer temperatures—oats, millet and flax. Moreover, they now have the ard, a kind of plough (*page 130*) that enables them to till expanded acreage.

The life style described in this imaginary village was typical of other Bronze Age Scandinavian communities. Aware of their blessings, the Northmen did everything they could think of to perpetuate the earth's fruitfulness. Ards were in fact so important to their sense of well-being that the implements became objects of reverence. In what is now the Swedish province of Bohuslaen, the ancient farmers immortalized one ard by carving it on a rock (*page 72*); it is shown in action, with ploughman and oxen in the middle of a furrowed field. And in both Sweden and Denmark, ards often were thrown into bogs as religious offerings, to be found thousands of years later by archaeologists. The sacrificial ards, however, were made of soft, easily carved wood, indicating that they were tokens; doubtless the real, workaday versions of the ard were made of sturdier material.

The presence of the ard in both the rock drawing and the bogs suggests certain changes in the Northmen's religious concepts. Though fertility may have continued to be a central concern, it was now a fertility associated with farming rather than with hunting. Instead of sacrificing animals to ensure a continued supply of game, the Northmen were now sacrificing objects identified with a productive harvest. Nothing supports this thesis more graphically

Designed to inspire awe, this bronze helmet unearthed at Viksoe in Denmark boasts curved horns and two staring eyes. The four-inch-high kneeling figure in Danish costume (right) wears a similar helmet, suggesting that such a head-piece was an important adjunct to the allure of a Bronze Age warrior.

*Braided tresses shorn from blonde women
in Denmark some 3,000 years ago now
have a tawny hue; the colour comes from
chemicals in peat bogs, into which the
hair was tossed—possibly as part
of a marriage, birth or death ritual.*

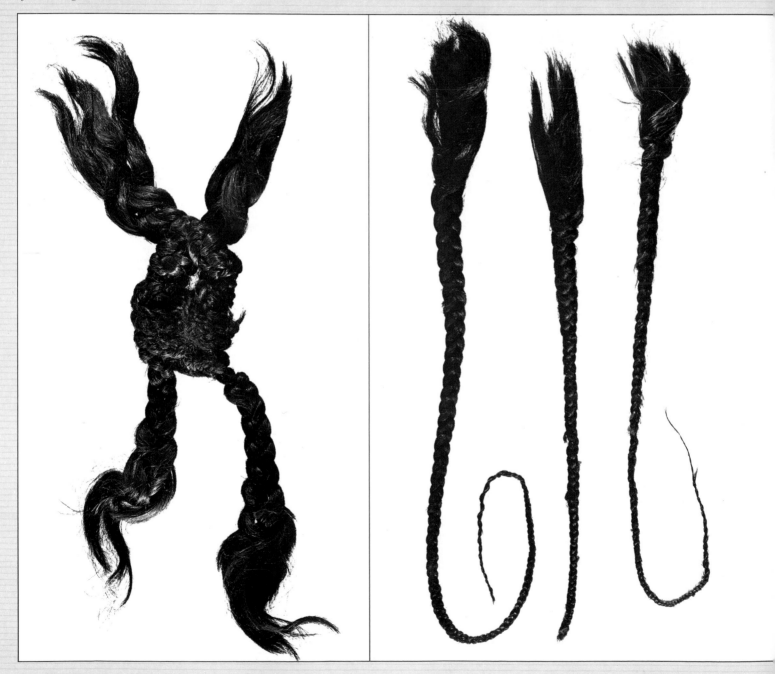

than the Bohuslaen rock carving of the ithyphallic Swedish ploughman portrayed at his labour; it is a powerful invocation of fertility. Perhaps the drawing was part of a spring planting ritual, a possibility heightened by the presence of many similarly earthy rock drawings, involving both males and females, on hillsides facing what were once Bronze Age fields and pastures. Sometimes the engravings are quite explicit —of mating couples, for instance. Sometimes the carvings are so cryptic that their meanings can only be guessed at. Many scholars consider the mysterious hollowed-out circles, called cup marks, to be sex symbols, though others think they may have been used to hold offerings.

A religious purpose for the rock carvings is also strongly suggested by the places in which they are found. Their moody settings on hillsides and cliff faces, glacier-scarred and pocked with mossy boulders, evoke a feeling of hallowed ground. To such sanctuaries may have flocked members of a cult. Near the ithyphallic ploughman is a drawing of two battling warriors. Do they represent war? Or are they perhaps actors in a ritual drama, representing winter and summer locked in perpetual struggle? There is also a drawing of a ship's crew, arms upraised, kneeling in the hull of their ship; one can almost hear them chanting. Are they worshipping the sun?

Now and then something tangible turns up to dramatize the underlying reality of such prehistoric scenes. The lurs—those great bronze trumpets that have been recovered from so many bogs—appear in the ancient rock drawings, raised to the lips of human figures. Not only can these ancient intruments now be held in the hands, but they can still be sounded some 3,000 years after they were made—and their mournful wail helps make the various sacred rituals at which they were played seem suddenly close.

Since lurs often are found with the bones of animals, and sometimes even with human remains, most scholars assume that they were blown at sacrificial rites and then were themselves sacrificed. It is inconceivable that the lurs could have been thrown into the bogs for any but religious reasons. Simply as metal, they are much too valuable. A matching pair unearthed at Stavanger, once the heart of Norway's Bronze Age culture, had been placed out in the open on a patch of marshy ground and left there until the moss and swamp grasses covered them over with what eventually became a layer of peat. That they had not been removed by Northmen who saw them lying there is clear proof of the lurs' sacred status.

A different sort of ritual, connected with light, warmth and rebirth, probably lies behind another major find: a miniature sun chariot (*pages 96-97*). This exquisite object—a bronze vehicle containing a gold-sheathed disc pulled by a beautiful bronze horse —was discovered in 1902 by a farmer ploughing his field near Trundholm in northern Zealand. The horse was used as a toy by the farmer's little girl until word of its existence reached the National Museum in Copenhagen, where it is now on display. As examples of the Bronze Age smith's aesthetic sense and technical skill, the horse and chariot represent a truly magnificent achievement.

If the Trundholm chariot is indeed a cult object connected with sun worship—its wheels correspond to rock drawings of identical wheels that have long been assumed to stand for sun symbols—then perhaps the Bronze Age Northmen, enlarging on the earlier farmers' belief in a mother goddess, also ven-

Fashions for the Ages

During the last century, excavations in Danish peat bogs have yielded an unsurpassed treasure of marvellously preserved prehistoric clothing, some of it more than 3,000 years old. With few exceptions, the fabrics seem to have been sheep's wool. Of various weights and textures, they were cut with a knife (scissors were not introduced into Scandinavia until about 300 B.C.) and then sewn into garments that were warm, practical and—in their simplicity—timelessly attractive.

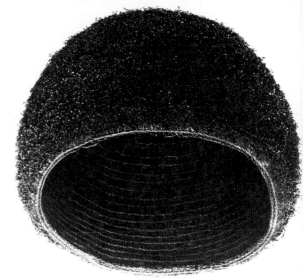

This Bronze Age man's cap consists of strips of felt.

Brow and hair covered with wool cords, the head of a young woman was sketched as found in 1935 in a 3,500-year-old oak coffin in southern Jutland. Buried in a cow-hide, she wore gold spiral earrings, a jacket, a skirt and leather shoes.

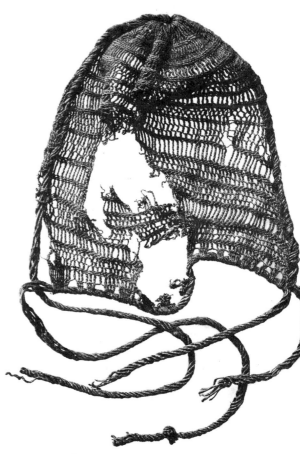

Extra-fine wool went into this braided hair net.

These 2,500-year-old garments, removed intact from a peat bog, are technically more sophisticated than earlier Bronze Age clothing. The plaid skirt (left) was produced by weaving contrasting wools, while the lines of the cowled dress (right) were influenced by Greek designs.

erated a sun god. And perhaps, like the Greek god Apollo, the Scandinavian sun god travelled across the heavens to sink into the land of the dead each evening and to rise into the land of the living each morning—hence the symbol of the horse pulling the sun, the golden disc, in the chariot.

The existence of a sun god in the Northmen's pantheon is also suggested by rock carvings of ships bearing similar discs. One scholar has suggested that these ships, too, were symbolic means of transport for the sun: from the moment it sank below the western horizon until it rose again in the east, the sun of Norse mythology may have journeyed by ship through the world of the night. If the Northmen did believe this, it would help to explain why they so often associated ships with burial: just as the solar ships returned the sun to the sky, so the grave ships may have carried the dead to some sort of rebirth.

By the close of the Bronze Age, some dead were being interred in stone-lined graves in the shapes of ships (*page 81*), just as many centuries later Viking noblemen were laid to rest in actual ships that served as coffins. Such burial ceremonies suggest a belief that ships carried the dead on a journey that ended, like the journey of the sun god across the heavens, in rebirth and a new life.

If the rock drawings, the lurs, the Trundholm chariot and the stone boats have ritual connotations that can only be guessed at, at least there is another relic that sheds light on one Scandinavian Bronze Age ceremony. It is a stone burial chamber whose slab sides are engraved with a series of pictures. The chamber is part of a rock cairn near the village of Kivik in southern Sweden (*page 117*). Stone cairns of this type were often constructed during the Bronze Age in re-

gions where there was apparently too little turf to justify using earth for barrows. The Kivik cairn is enormous, measuring more than 255 feet in diameter. (The chamber itself measures only 13 feet long and three feet wide.) In fact, the cairn was used as a quarry until the middle of the 18th Century when two farmers, raiding it for building materials, came upon the burial chamber. The tomb was quickly plundered of its valuables, but one treasure remained: the engravings on the stone slabs.

There can be little doubt that the carvings depict ceremonies, and little doubt too, considering the setting, that the ceremonies have to do with the dead. Here are a whole series of horses, ships and sun wheels, arranged symmetrically and in pairs. Here are people in robes strung out in a procession: a man driving a wagon, a charioteer, and trumpeters blowing lurs. Although the burial took place in southern Sweden, 400 miles away from the mound in Denmark where the young woman of Egtved was interred, the Danish funeral may have been composed of some of the same elements, and thus can be imagined.

Perhaps the funeral begins at the home of the Egtved girl with a series of ritual sacrifices conducted by her family or a priest. Then the solemn procession of mourners forms, the lurs sound the dirge and the body of the girl, lying on its cowhide shroud, is placed on a horse-drawn bier. Slowly the procession winds along the narrow main road leading out of the village, past the low hills dominated by the burial mounds of previous generations. And now a new mound has been added. For days the workers have been preparing the site. Sections of turf have been lifted, a bed of stones has been laid down to receive

When this drawing was made in the late 18th Century, the stone cairn—or burial mound—at Kivik in Sweden was being used as a quarry. Today it is considered one of the most revealing funeral monuments of the Bronze Age in Europe. Its sepulchral chamber contains 10 slabs, six of which depict funeral rites; the one seen here, now missing and believed to form part of a local cottage's chimney, bore carvings of two axes, an obelisk and, along its bottom, either a boat or sledge.

the casket, and the massive oak coffin itself has been hewed and hollowed on the spot from a trunk, the white chips left where they fell on the earth.

Only a person of high rank or considerable wealth could command such a burial. Dressed in finery, the girl has been carefully groomed. Her fingernails have been cleaned and trimmed, and her blonde hair dressed and tied back with a ribbon.

As the bier reaches the burial ground, the young woman's body is lifted and placed in its coffin, and two birch-bark boxes are laid beside it. One is a small work box containing her effects: a bronze awl, a few bronze pins and a length of woollen cord—perhaps an extra hair ribbon. The other box contains a ritual token of remembrance from her survivors: a drink made from the fermented juices of various berries that grow in bogs. And at her feet the mourners place a small cloth-wrapped bundle, the cremated remains of a seven- or eight-year-old child. Perhaps the dead child, too, is a ritual gesture, a sacrificial offering made in honour of the young woman's high station. Perhaps the cremated remains are simply those of a young member of the clan who has recently died and is sharing in the funeral.

And now all is ready. The cow-hide shroud is folded over the body, and someone steps forward (her husband? her mother?) to drop in the last token: the sprig of yarrow. The coffin lid is closed and the crowd departs, but the interment continues for days. Stones are piled on the coffin to keep out grave robbers and animals. Great masses of turf are stripped from the surrounding meadows to be placed in layers on top of the stones. Gradually the new barrow rises on top of its hill, there to stand for 3,500 years, a monument to a much-esteemed young woman and to the golden age in which she lived.

Prized Possessions of an Affluent Society

The sparkle and brilliance of certain metals have immemorially delighted men of all cultures, and the Northmen were no exception. As the exchange of goods accelerated between an increasingly prosperous Scandinavia and the rest of Europe during the Second Millennium B.C., more and more traders and tinkers brought alluring items of bronze and gold to the Northlands.

At first the Scandinavians seemed content to import only finished products. But, with the help of foreign master craftsmen, they themselves learned the secrets of metalworking. Soon all over Denmark and southern Sweden native smiths became expert at combining tin and copper into bronze, and then casting it and gold into intricate and beautiful jewellery like the torque, or neck ring, shown here. Within a few centuries their work reflected such a high degree of technical and artistic sophistication that the results equalled and often surpassed those of their mentors to the south.

Gleaming like gold, this tension-sprung collar is made of cast bronze, worked while still soft into an intricate double-twist design.

Masterpieces of the Jeweller's Craft

The Northmen's earliest attempts at bronze and gold jewellery were little more than clumsy imitations of fine work executed by master smiths in central and southern Europe. But as Scandinavian skills flowered, the Northmen evolved rich designs apparently all their own. Foremost among the motifs was the spiral, which, some scholars suggest, symbolizes, in its endless coiling, eternity or the infinite. The Northmen used the spiral both as a form in itself (rings, near right) and as surface decoration (bronze brooch at far right below).

Two coiled rings of gold—dated around 800 B.C.—seem modern.

Gold earrings clung to lobes from the tension created by their shape.

Two pins of gold and bronze, both more than seven inches long, date from 600 B.C.

This late Bronze Age gold bracelet—reproduced here about twice its actual size—terminates in four delicately executed spirals.

Reproduced life size, this bronze brooch from a Danish grave is covered with gold foil and decorated with minutely incised spirals.

Treasures from Abroad

Although the Northmen came to excel at casting bronze or gold, they never achieved mastery of the techniques for hammered metalwork. The art of beating metal into paper-thin sheets. shaping them into desired forms and then ornamenting them with designs punched from the inside had been perfected by central Europeans. The Northmen so admired the work that they imported countless hammered vases and bowls, such as the ones on these pages, probably to use as votive offerings. More than 40 such pieces have been found in Denmark alone.

This 2,500-year-old gold cup was recovered in almost pristine condition from a bog. Though the five-inch-wide bowl had been imported from central Europe, the handle was added locally.

A golden bowl from the late Bronze Age is embellished with delicate concentric circles, ribbing and beading (below). The thinness of the metal can best be seen from overhead (left). The bowl is about seven inches wide.

Just over four inches tall, this hammered gold vase was buried deep in a hill on Zealand along with much other golden treasure.

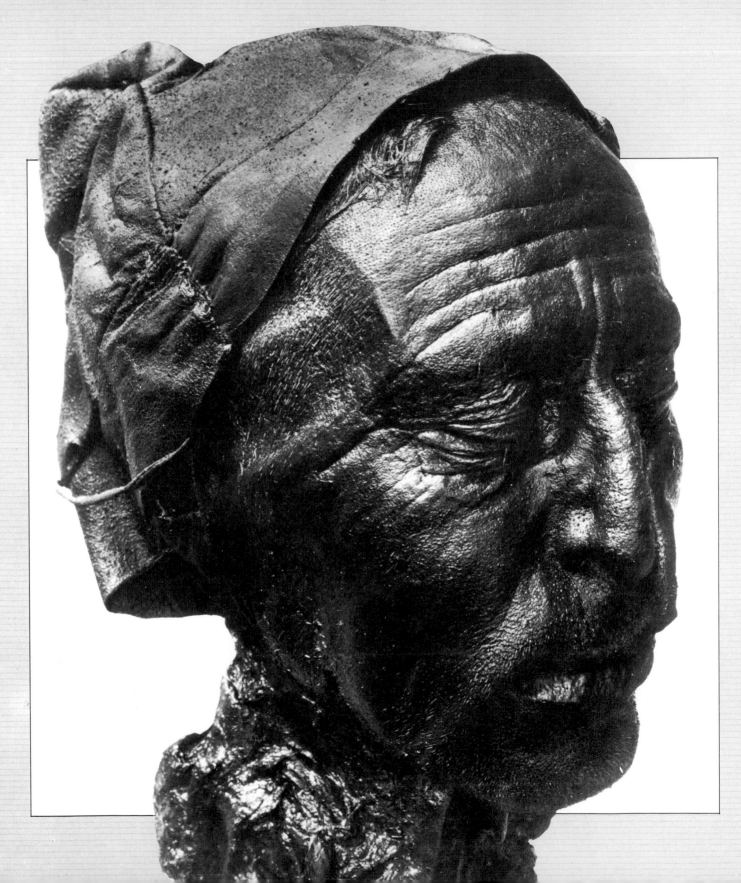

Around 500 B.C. the halcyon days of the Bronze Age, the greatest period of Scandinavian prehistory, came to an end. The age would be remembered later as a time when Scandinavian craftsmanship in gold and bronze surpassed that of other Europeans, when Scandinavian ships and seafarers threaded the northern seas, when the bodies of prosperous Scandinavians were interred with treasure in massive burial mounds. "Of gold no lack did the gods then know" runs one proud line in a poem from the *Edda*.

Why did the splendour fade? A shift in climate from warm to cool radically altered for the worse the character of the Scandinavian environment. Simultaneously, the introduction of ironwork into the north disrupted the Northmen's bronze-based economy, and the Celts' rise to dominance in central Europe cut Scandinavia's trade connections with the south. Together, these circumstances tested the Northmen's ability not merely to adapt but to survive.

The changes the two occurrences brought about began in little ways that at first must have seemed only curious to the Northmen—if indeed they were perceptible at all. Towards the close of the Bronze Age, for instance, from about 900 to 500 B.C., fewer and fewer great burial mounds were built, reflecting a levelling out of the social order. Little by little, people were turning to cremation, and they buried the bones and ashes in pits marked only by stone

Tollund man, named after the region around the Danish peat bog where he was discovered in 1950, wears an expression more like sleep than death. He was strangled or hanged and lowered into the bog as a sacrifice about 200 B.C. His body was so well preserved that doctors could perform an autopsy on it; examination of the stomach revealed that his last meal, perhaps a ceremonial dinner, had contained various seeds.

slabs or rings of stones—modest memorials that were quickly overgrown and forgotten.

The slow pace at which one form of burial replaced another rules out conjecture that recent arrivals brought a new religion with new customs. And in any case, cremation was an alternative form of burial even in the early Bronze Age; witness the burnt bones of the child interred with the young woman of Egtved. But the eventual adoption of cremation as a regular practice does suggest a change in people's feelings about life and the afterlife—a change, perhaps, from a materialistic to a more spiritual view of the world of the dead. The body may now have been regarded as no more than a perishable receptacle for the spirit, and the destruction of the body as a release of the spirit; carried upwards on the flames of the funeral pyre, the soul ascended to the gods. Some such concept may account for the presence in one late Bronze Age cremation urn of three pairs of wings from jackdaws and one pair from a crow—the black birds of death. The wings may have been included to help the spirit on its skywards journey.

Another sign of changing times in the Northlands was a decline in the bronzesmith's art. With the growing acceptance of cremation, the demand for rich grave goods lessened. Since the flames consumed clothing and offerings along with the body, the objects that went into the burial urns—when placed there at all—were small and of little value. Bronze treasures did continue to be thrown into bogs as gifts for the gods, but even these sacrifices lacked the elegance and refinement of former times; the ritual torques and brooches had grown in size and weight out of all proportion to their function (*pages 128-129*), and the belt discs and arm rings were so gross that they could scarcely have been worn with comfort, much less with grace.

As for the splendid bronze daggers and swords, supreme examples of the northern bronzesmith's art, they were now being replaced by weapons of iron. Even when forged in exactly the same shapes as their Bronze Age prototypes, the new weapons looked dull and clumsy. But then, they were not meant for show: their sole purpose was to maim and kill, and that they did well. A bronze sword with too much tin in it could break and one with too little tin could bend. But an iron sword—one that was hardened by having carbon pounded into it—took a keen and durable cutting edge. With such a weapon a warrior could throw his full weight into a devastating series of cuts and slashes with no fear that his weapon would bend or shatter in his hands.

Whoever possessed iron possessed the means to lord it over all those who did not. The Celts, a people whose culture originated in central Europe, began to switch from bronze to iron around 1000 B.C., and in 500 years they were able to dominate a swath of Europe that stretched from the Black Sea to the Atlantic shores of Ireland.

The first Celtic ironwork to enter Scandinavia appeared at the height of the Bronze Age, but it was not until about 500 B.C. that the Northmen themselves learned the secret of forging iron, and launched an Iron Age of their own. At that, their accomplishments were based on Celtic technology and design, for though the Scandinavians were superb craftsmen in bronze, they could not begin to match the Celts in the working of iron. The Celts in fact continued to supply the models for northern metalsmiths right up to the beginning of the Christian era, when

Roman influence, and Roman artisans, reached the boundaries of Scandinavia.

But if Iron Age Scandinavian smiths lacked the skills of their Bronze Age forbears, they had one advantage: a ready supply of raw material. Unlike bronze, which depended for its manufacture on imported copper and tin, iron could be found almost everywhere in Scandinavia, including Denmark. Even today the mountains of Sweden are noted for their excellent ore. In prehistoric times the common source of the metal in Scandinavia was bog iron. Constantly seeping out of the earth to collect in layers in peat bogs, bog iron could be turned into perfectly acceptable tools and weapons.

The easy availability of iron to the common man threatened the very foundations of Scandinavia's wealthy class, whose power had rested largely upon control of the bronze trade and the bronze industry. But iron alone did not destroy Scandinavia's Bronze Age society. The decisive blow seems in fact to have been dealt by the Celts who, in the course of spreading across central Europe, had interfered with the long-established trade routes running from Scandinavia to the Mediterranean. The focus for the highly profitable amber trade shifted, for instance, from Denmark to the eastern shores of the Baltic. Circumventing the Celts, amber now moved south along the Vistula and Dnieper rivers to the Black Sea, and from there into the Aegean. Thus Scandinavia abruptly lost its thousand-year-old connection with the Mediterranean world.

With this sudden loss of trade, Scandinavia's economy faltered and the clear distinctions between rich and poor began to disappear—with everyone eventually receiving the same humble burial.

Bones of the dead once filled this 10-inch-high pottery cremation urn designed to resemble a round house with a little door. Though the house-shaped urn occurs only in southern Sweden and Denmark, cremation urns from the late Bronze Age have cropped up all over Scandinavia, showing how widespread the practice of cremating bodies had become.

Meanwhile, a new social order apparently had emerged in the Northlands. Very likely certain artisans, such as metalworkers, continued to occupy privileged places in Iron Age society. But by and large the Northmen's way of life no longer allowed for the class distinctions of the Bronze Age. Now everyone had to pull his own weight, and from all indications people had to labour much harder than before. Tilling the soil and tending cattle were efforts to which almost everyone contributed, simply because the land itself, through over use and other factors, had become impoverished.

This turn of events, compounding the economic decline, was caused by a sudden and devastating deterioration in climate. The change seems to have begun around 500 B.C., just as the Iron Age started. Apparently it was triggered by a shift in ocean currents and in the intensity of the sun's radiation. From the luxuriant warmth characteristic of the Bronze Age the weather turned cold and wet. Over the course of only a few hundred years, perhaps only a few generations, summer became a time of wind and rain and fog, and winter a time of darkness, of drifting snow and bitter cold.

In the uplands of the Scandinavian peninsula glaciers reappeared and the tree line moved down the mountainsides as much as a thousand feet. Along coastal Norway the woods vanished, leaving the Norwegian shoreline as treeless as it is today. The fir, the Scotch pine and the beech, now so typical of the Scandinavian landscape, overran the oak forests of the Bronze Age. And in many places torrents of rain water leached the life from the soil, formed bogs and swamp, and drowned fields and pastures.

The course of these climatological events can be traced today in the Scandinavian subsoil. A definite layer marks the places where the nutrients washed from the earth, leaving heather to spread unchecked on land that could no longer support trees and crops. Similarly, in the bogs a reddish layer of spongy, water-absorbent sphagnum moss (known in Denmark as dog's flesh because of its colour) stands out from the dense, dark layers formed by rotted tree stumps and other vegetation.

Another clear indication of how the worsening cli-

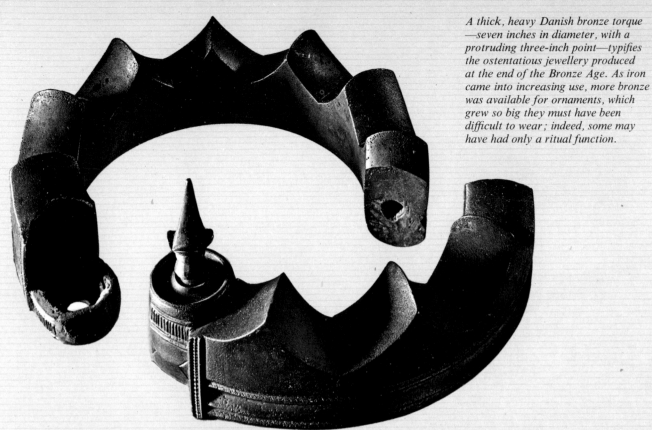

mate challenged the Northmen is offered by archaeology. Although the hunting peoples of the far north were little affected by the sudden cold, many of the farmers and herdsmen living farther south were forced to retreat from their lands. In Norway, for example, almost all traces of farming settlements disappear from the archaeological record, except in low-lying coastal areas.

Even in more congenial regions the weather was too harsh to encourage easy living. This is clear from the remains of early Iron Age houses that have been found all over southern Scandinavia: solid, weather-tight structures built of stone and earth in Sweden and Norway and of turf in Denmark, some with walls as much as three feet thick. Today all that is left of these dwellings are their foundations—ridges of earth only a few inches high, scarcely noticeable except for the shadows they cast in the slanting rays of the morning or evening sun.

In the worsening climate, the livestock had to be given shelter. No longer could animals be kept out-doors during winter—as they had been in the Bronze Age—without either freezing to death or starving when snow buried their pastures. Now cattle, pigs, horses and sheep had to be brought indoors, often right into the houses.

Providing fodder for these animals as well as food for his family must have presented the Iron Age farmer with a never-ending task. When the weather was not cold, it was apt to be damp. On many a morning he must have stood in his doorway, looking out at fields laid waste by wind and drenching rain. No doubt he was often tempted to join those of his neighbours who were abandoning their farms in the hope of finding better acreage elsewhere, or who were banding together to plunder the herds and food supplies of other settlements. The Iron Age was a period of increasing tension and strife, one in which the seafaring Northmen built their great war canoes, and the first wave of northern invaders, the Cimbri and Teutons, descended upon western Europe and moved south for their historic confrontation with Rome.

More light is shed on the Northmen—and their reactions to the depressing climate—by Roman authors. In A.D. 98 Tacitus noted, for example, that the harsh weather and poor soil of their homeland in-

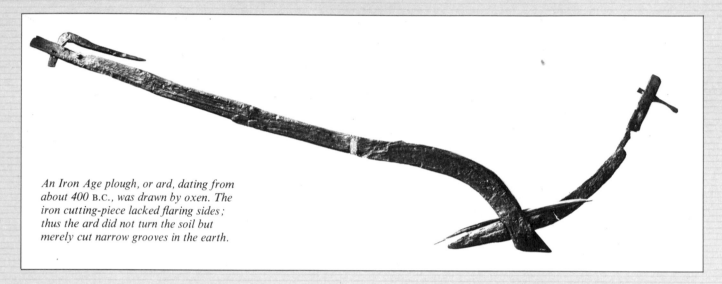

An Iron Age plough, or ard, dating from about 400 B.C., was drawn by oxen. The iron cutting-piece lacked flaring sides; thus the ard did not turn the soil but merely cut narrow grooves in the earth.

ured the Northmen to cold and hunger, and made them skilled and fearless warriors. They had no taste for peace, he observed, and never went unarmed, no matter what business they were transacting. But the carrying of arms was strictly controlled. No young man was permitted to bear arms until the elders of his tribe was satisfied that he was competent to use them, and consequently, there was no greater honour for a young man than to receive his first shield and spear. "These," Tacitus wrote, "are the equivalent of the man's toga with us."

Next to warfare the Northmen loved eating, drinking, gambling and carousing; and for the boldest and most warlike men, these pursuits were apt to constitute daily activities. "As soon as they wake," Tacitus reported, "which is often well after sunrise, they wash, generally with warm water—as one might expect in a country where winter lasts so long. After washing they eat a meal . . . Then they go out to attend to any business they have in hand, or, as often

as not, to partake in a feast—always with their weapons about them. Drinking bouts lasting all day and all night are not considered in any way disgraceful."

Yet, despite this intemperance, Tacitus found the Northmen attractive in many ways. They were, for instance, enormously generous hosts. "It is accounted a sin to turn a man away from your door. The host welcomes his guest with the finest meal that his means allow. When he had finished entertaining him, the host undertakes a fresh rôle: he accompanies the guest to the nearest house where further hospitality can be had. It makes no difference that they come uninvited; they are welcomed just as warmly."

Tacitus was also impressed by the Northmen's strict marriage code, "and no feature of their morality deserves higher praise". "They are," he wrote, "almost unique among barbarians in being content with one wife apiece." Women were regarded as possessing "an element of holiness and a gift of prophecy; and so they do not scorn their advice, or lightly disregarded their replies". And in marriage, said Tacitus, it was the man who supplied the dowry; his gifts consisted of oxen, a horse and bridle, perhaps a shield, a spear and a sword. The woman's bridal gift to her husband was customarily weapons, signifying her willingness to enter his household "to be the partner of his toils and perils".

In describing the Northmen's villages Tacitus spoke of many things that have been confirmed by the field work of modern archaeologists. He noted, for instance, that the houses were detached, with open spaces around them—a building plan quite unlike the one used in Roman villages. He thought the open spaces might have been intended "perhaps as a precaution against the risk of fire", and archaeologists have proved that he was right.

Similarly, Tacitus reported that the Northmen had "the habit of hollowing out underground caves, which they cover with masses of manure and use both as refuges . . . and as storage for produce". On this score, too, he is substantially correct. At several sites in Denmark archaeologists have uncovered the remains of what were apparently root cellars: oval chambers several feet below ground littered with shards of storage jars. The chambers show signs of having been lived in temporarily, perhaps in times of danger—just as Tacitus said.

Inevitably, of course, the work of modern archaeologists has greatly enlarged the picture of the Northmen presented by Tacitus and other classical authors. From unprepossessing Scandinavian habitation sites, for instance, they have been able to deduce not only the architecture of the houses, but also a good bit of information about what went on in them and in the surrounding fields. They know, for example, that the houses were laid out on a long narrow floor plan, with a double row of posts down the middle to support the roof—just as in the dwellings of the much earlier Barkaer farmers. They know that there was commonly a hearth at the west end of the house, where the people lived, and that the cattle, horses, chickens and sheep were usually quartered at the east end. They know that the furnishings included pottery dishes and jars, looms and weaving stolls, and stone querns for grinding grain. They even know—from a set of weights found on an earthen floor—that in some houses fish nets must have festooned the rafters.

In many places in southern Scandinavia archaeologists have plotted the actual fields in which iron Age farmers grew grain and other foodstuffs. The boundaries of the fields are marked by piles of stones that were removed from the soil preparatory to planting it, or by mounds of earth—called balks—created at the ends of the furrows by the turning plough. By painstakingly lifting and dusting the soil between the balks, archaeologists have even uncovered the lines of the ancient furrows—lines inscribed where the dark topsoil was driven down into the lighter subsoil by the blades of the ploughs.

One of the richest of the Iron Age sites is at Borremose fen in northern Jutland (*page 138*). Here, on what used to be a small island in the middle of a marshy plain, archaeologists have turned up the remains of a fortified Iron Age village built in the first century before Christ. From the surrounding area have come other important finds. In a near-by bog the bodies of two women and a man were uncovered in the late 1940s. Preserved so well by the acids in the peat that it seemed to their discoverers they might have been alive only recently, the bodies were in fact contemporary with the village at Borremose fen —perhaps three of its inhabitants.

A half century earlier, near Borremose fen in 1891, peat cutters had stumbled on one of the great treasures of antiquity: the Gundestrup silver cauldron (*pages 133-136*), embossed with pictures of gods and goddesses, animal combat and human sacrifice. Most scholars think that the cauldron is Celtic in workmanship and that it was brought to the area as a trophy by returning tribesmen—perhaps by the very Cimbrian warriors who terrorized Rome. The Cimbri are thought to have come from the part of Jutland where it was found; perhaps they were even the relatives or neighbours of the people of Borremose fen.

Like the earlier settlers at Barkaer, these villagers must have chosen their island site with security in mind. A narrow causeway leading across the marsh made the settlement easy to defend, but for added protection an earthen rampart and a wooden palisade rimmed the island's perimeter, one of the earliest-known defence works in northern Europe. Inside stood 20 houses, orientated east to west and grouped around a single paved street leading to the causeway. The houses varied in size, but all had thick turf walls. Probably the structures were roofed with layers of thatch, the eaves hanging almost to the ground. Although there was some open space around the houses for cattle and perhaps a garden plot or two, the main fields and pastures lay across the causeway, on the firm ground beyond the marsh.

The discovery of the village site provided much information about the Northmen's way of life during the Iron Age. But now there is another kind of in-

formation available. In recent years Scandinavian archaeologists have broken new ground. From facts collected at Borremose fen and other sites, they have evolved an imaginative technique for studying the Iron Age—re-creating it. Twenty-five miles west of Copenhagen they have established a research centre where archaeological information has been put to the test. Here, they have taken the idea first put forth by Jens Worsaae a century ago—that of taking the study of prehistory out of the museum and into the field —and have carried it to extraordinary lengths.

The research centre is near the village of Lejre, identified in Norse sagas as the legendary seat of Denmark's ancient kings (*pages 23-33*). Established in 1964 and supported by a private foundation, the Lejre centre is in effect a workshop where archaeologists can use the precise methods of experimental science to verify otherwise imprecise notions of the way people lived 2,000 years ago. Given the archaeological evidence of how Iron Age houses were laid out and their walls built, what could be discovered about the roof construction? How thick did the thatch have to be to keep out the wind and cold? What was the safest size for an open-hearth fire in a thatch-roofed house, and would such a fire keep the house warm in the dead of winter? How was pottery made and at what temperature was it fired? How many bushels of grain could be harvested from the crudely ploughed earth of a typical Iron Age field?

Starting from what they knew about the construction of the ancient houses, and using copies of ancient adzes and axes, the scientists built a group of wattle-and-daub dwellings, with roofs of varying pitch, covered with thatch, reeds, heather or turf. They soon discovered that the houses had to be a certain size

Text continued on page 137

For the Spirits of the Bogs, a Silver Cauldron

In 1891, in a remote part of Jutland, a peat cutter laid bare a portion of the most dazzling ancient treasure ever unearthed in Denmark: the silver Gundestrup cauldron, named after the township in which is was found. Over the intervening years, the two-foot-wide cauldron has proved to be as much an enigma as a cause for awe. To most scholars, the staring faces, the weird scenes and the animals that adorn it mark the cauldron as the work of Celtic craftsmen. Just where it was made—possibly France or central Europe—is uncertain; how it found its way to Denmark is even more perplexing. P. V. Glob, director of the Danish National Museum, where the cauldron now resides, speculates that it was a trophy sent home by Denmark's Cimbrian warriors fighting in far-off Celtic lands. The only thing certain about its history is that the early Danes dismantled its plates and laid the pieces on the bog as a sacrifice to their gods.

The embossed Gundestrup cauldron, painstakingly reassembled and restored, shows few signs of its 2,000-year immersion in a Danish bog.

In this detail from the Gundestrup cauldron, three soldiers—to the right of the two-row military procession—blow wolf-headed trumpets. At le

large figure dangles a smaller one over a vessel in what may be a bloodletting sacrifice—reflecting, perhaps, the original use of the cauldron.

*In another scene from the cauldron, a god, framed by wild
animals, performs a long-lost ritual. In his left hand he holds
a serpent and in his right a torque similar to the one around
his neck. The stag antlers on his head probably symbolize virility.*

—at least 12 to 20 feet wide and 10 to 13 feet high. A roof less than 10 feet high was too close to the open hearth for safety, and one more than 13 feet high was too lofty for proper smoke removal. And even within these critical limits there were problems. Any fire that blazed higher than 20 inches was dangerous, the scientists discovered; so were fires made of materials like twigs and straw, because they sent up sparks and floating embers that ignited the thatch.

The long-held assumption that the houses had been vented with some sort of smoke hole directly above the hearth turned out to be false. The hole not only let in rain, it provided too little draught to draw the smoke upwards. As a solution, the researchers cut two openings in the gable ends of the houses, and fitted these with louvered vents. Though the resulting cross-current did not remove all the smoke, it did at least make the air within the houses breathable. Furthermore, the smoke in the loft kept away bugs and rodents, which made the attic a good place for storing grain and for curing meat and fish.

Volunteers who lived in one of the vented houses through part of one winter quickly found that a safe fire provided precious little heat. As soon as they stepped away from the hearth they shivered. And thermometers placed in various parts of the house confirmed their responses: temperatures were often below freezing. Some additional warmth was supplied by a clay-and-wattle heating oven, modelled on a type found at several Iron Age sites. Also, the volunteers discovered that the livestock with which they shared the house as part of the normal Iron Age pattern of living provided, through their body heat, another welcome source of warmth. Having thus raised the indoor temperature, the participants in the experiment made the house a bit more liveable by spreading out the thatch more evenly over the roof.

Turning to other kinds of experiments, the scientists planted crops like those of Iron Age farmers —millet, six-row barley, and emmer and einkorn wheat. To till the fields they used copies of the Iron Age plough—the ard (*page 130*)—hitched to oxen and horses that had been brought from northern Scandinavia and Iceland. The animals approximated Iron Age stock in size and build.

In the pottery workshop researchers duplicated the clay mixtures of prehistoric potters and made replicas of the ancient wares so accurate that they had to introduce flaws deliberately in order to mark the copies as forgeries. In the weaving workshop, other researchers learned to spin wool into the exact thickness and strength of Iron Age thread. They duplicated the upright, warp-weighted loom used by the ancient weavers and wove and sewed exact copies of the clothes that had been found on bodies in the bogs. They even went to the trouble of submerging samples of their textiles in the bogs, to see if the changes in the fibres and colours would correspond to those found in the originals.

Through such experiments Lejre has vividly introduced modern Scandinavians to their past; indeed, the centre functions not only as a research facility but also as a school. In one four-year period, for instance, 300 teachers were trained in the old methods of spinning and weaving, and they in turn passed on their knowledge to Danish school children—6,000 to 8,000 of them a year. Other workshops at Lejre have conducted similar training programmes.

But the chief function of Lejre remains research. And when the information gained from the exper-

iments is matched with the archaeological evidence of an Iron Age settlement like Borremose fen, a remarkable picture emerges. Walking through the ruins of Borremose fen on a chilly autumn evening, passing the heaps of earth that mark the erstwhile walls of its houses, one can forget the neat modern farms lying near by and see instead the village—a village like Lejre—that stood here 2,000 years ago. The smoke curls upwards from the louvered openings in the gables; inside the houses the cattle have been bedded down, while the people assemble around their hearths for their evening meal.

It has been a long day. In the fields the men have been harvesting hay and grain, hoping to get the crop under cover before the cold and damp cause it to rot on the ground. They wear coats and short capes of wool or fur to keep out the chill and protect themselves from intermittent drizzles; some have on leggings and others pants—an article of clothing used by the nomadic horsemen of central Asia and recently introduced to the Northlands. Each man works his own plot and will someday—if the soil holds out—divide his plot among his sons.

At midday the men squat down on the mounds of earth at the edges of their fields to rest and eat, drinking from clay vessels. Broken bits of pottery from their past meals lie among the stones, there to remain until archaeologists 2,000 years later dig them up. After the noon-time break, it is back to work until the day's grey light begins to fade. Then sheaves of grain are loaded on the backs of cattle, sickles and rakes are shouldered, and a weary procession of men and animals heads home, picking its way single file along the narrow causeway.

On the island the women too have been busy. Rising with the sun to feed their children and menfolk, they then set about the business of preparing the winter's food supply. They thresh grain from the sheaves brought in the night before and store it in the big clay pots that stand along the walls of every house. This chore done, some of the women grind grain for bread; others bake bread or begin the fermentation processes that turn milk into cheese and grain into mead. At least one woman, turning over her regular tasks to her mother or daughters, spends the better part of the day making pots. The dishes, bowls, jars and drinking vessels that she turns out will be used by her immediate family and by those of her neighbours who have not yet become masters of the potter's art.

Another woman devotes most of her time to weaving, working at a loom that stands near the open doorway. By alternating light and dark wools at regular intervals, she achieves a monochromatic plaid. The cloth, when finished, will be made into an ankle-length dress for one of her daughters. Woven as a circular tube, the dress will be worn tied at the waist and folded outwards over the shoulders to form a cowl that not only can be pulled up over the head but may also be drawn around the body as a shawl (*page 115*).

At the close of the day, the women of Borremose fen hasten to the near-by spring singly and in pairs to fill their water jugs. As the men return, each family gathers about the fire for the evening meal. There are the murmur of voices, the smell of food: porridge, cheese, perhaps some roasted meat. Then, as the light fails, it is time to build up the fire and stretch out around it. There is much work to be done in preparation for winter. The men must cut peat and store it for the hearth fires before the ground becomes fro-

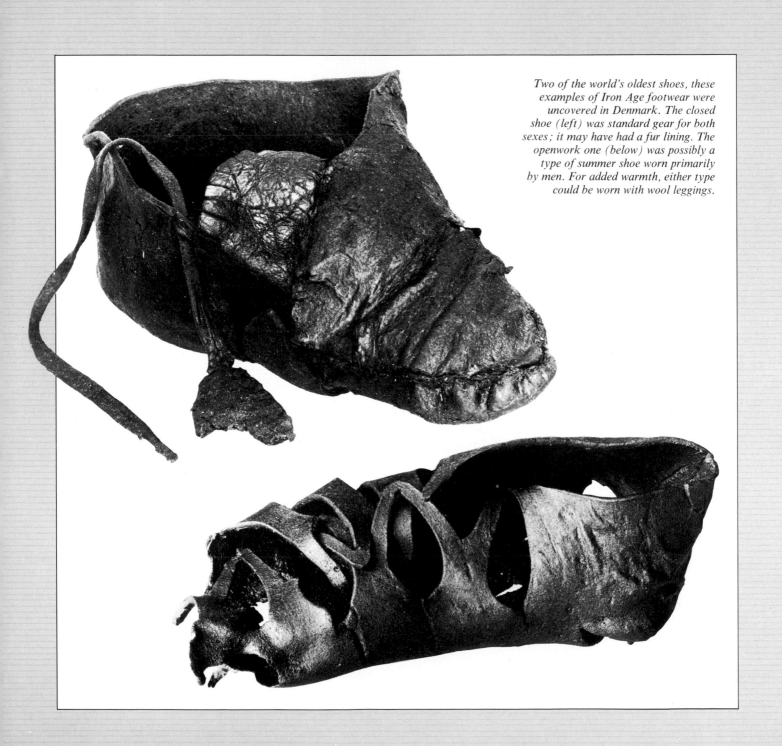

Two of the world's oldest shoes, these examples of Iron Age footwear were uncovered in Denmark. The closed shoe (left) was standard gear for both sexes; it may have had a fur lining. The openwork one (below) was possibly a type of summer shoe worn primarily by men. For added warmth, either type could be worn with wool leggings.

zen; with all arable land put to the plough, there are no longer great forests to draw upon for firewood. The women must continue to weave warm winter clothing and preserve food for winter.

It may have been on a night like this that one of the houses in the village met disaster. A door blew open, a few sparks escaped from the hearth and flew up into the thatch. Suddenly the house was in flames. The women grabbed the children and guided the older people to safety. The men scrambled to free the panicky animals before the flames engulfed them. In 10 or 15 minutes little remained of the house except smoking rubble.

Archaeologists have exposed the ashes of just such a blaze at Borremose fen, and similar discoveries have been made elsewhere. With their tinderbox roofs, Iron Age houses were highly vulnerable to fire. At some sites there is evidence of burning and rebuilding as many as five times. And often, leaping from roof to roof, the fire resulted in holocausts that destroyed whole villages. At Lejre, seeking to discover what the charred ruins uncovered at various sites could reveal about the dwellings themselves, researchers set ablaze some of the reconstructed houses and timed the progress of the fires. So quickly did the flames spread that the researchers concluded that the occupants could have had no more than two minutes to escape. One house burned to the ground in exactly 16 minutes.

There is evidence that at least one Iron Age family took steps against a repeat of disaster. Under their rebuilt house, which stood in a village that had been totally consumed by fire, an archaeologist uncovered an axe buried blade up, sharp edge towards the sky. To the finder the axe suggested a kind of fire prevention; lightning, he reasoned, must have caused many fires in the Iron Age; and the buried axe was a resort to magic: "a weapon turned against the weapon of the thunder, a cutting edge against a cutting edge".

At Borremose fen, however, the house that burned was not rebuilt and the ashes were left to lie. Possibly the survivors—if there were any—chose to rebuild elsewhere. Perhaps they were sheltered temporarily by neighbours. But if the fire occurred in winter and destroyed their cattle and food supplies, the disaster must have been catastrophic, placing a burden on everyone in the village.

Even under the best of circumstances winter was a cruel time in Iron Age Scandinavia. The season arrived early and stayed late. Ponds froze over, and so did springs. Wolves prowled close to villages in search of food, while indoors, huddled around their peat fires, families got by as best they could. Fresh food was nonexistent for months on end; the human bones and bodies found in the bogs show signs that many of the people suffered from malnutrition. In an effort to make stored food last as long as possible, men, women and children must have gone hungry often. Those least able to make do with meagre fare, the very young and the very old, no doubt suffered most and must have frequently sickened and died.

For the villagers of Borremose fen, spring, when it finally came, must have been welcome indeed. It may have been in anticipation of the season, while the days were beginning to lengthen but the earth was still barren, that they gathered at the near-by bog to offer sacrifices to the gods, to pray for the sun's warmth and the earth's fruitfulness.

During the Iron Age people made sacrifices as they

142

*This pile of bronze rings, approximately
350 of them, was recovered from a
wooden well enclosing a pure spring in
Jutland. Since springs in Denmark have
traditionally been associated with
fertility and good fortune, these women's
ornaments seem to have been Iron
Age gifts to a mother or earth goddess.*

had for thousands of years—swords, food, pottery, splendid offerings like the silver Gundestrup cauldron. But now, more than ever before, human beings were consigned to the bogs. Sometimes the sacrifices represented tokens of gratitude for favours to come: a bountiful harvest, a great victory in war. Sometimes they were attempts to even the score. Men and women who had offended the gods or who had transgressed the laws of the community were killed and placed in the bogs—not only to propitiate the gods but also as a convenient way of ridding the village of unwanted members.

There is no way of knowing for certain into which category the three Borremose fen bodies fit. But some fascinating hints about the victims emerge when the circumstances of their death are viewed in the light of Tacitus' writings. In his chapter on the laws of the northerners, Tacitus noted that punishment varied with the crime: "Traitors and deserters are hanged on trees; cowards, shirkers and sodomites are pressed down under a wicker hurdle into the slimy mud of a bog." The distinctions between punishments, Tacitus said, were based on the notion that "offenders against the state should be made a public example of, whereas deeds of shame should be buried out of men's sight". Tacitus also described the punishment meted out to a woman caught in adultery: her husband "cuts off her hair, strips her naked, and in the presence of her kinsmen turns her out of his house and flogs her all through the village"

Now it just so happens that two of the bodies recovered from the Borremose bog are naked—and all three victims met violent deaths. One of the women lay face downwards in the bog, a woollen blanket thrown carelessly over her. The back of her head was

shaved, her body battered, the front of her skull crushed as from a heavy blow. The attitude of her corpse—one leg drawn up beneath her, one hand raised to her shattered face—gives a vivid impression of her last half-conscious agony. The other woman had a crushed skull and a fractured left leg, and she too had been tossed into the bog face down; beside her were the bones of an infant. The man, short of stature, with a reddish stubble on his chin, had also been cruelly treated; one of his legs was broken above the knee and the back of his head was caved in. But the immediate cause of his death had been strangulation: around the man's neck was a length of hemp rope, caught through a slip knot. When found in the bog, his body was covered with branches, perhaps used to imprison him in the muck.

All three of these victims may have been guilty of some sort of tribal transgression. But they could just as well have played some part in a religious ritual. One of the common symbols of the fertility goddess, for instance, is a twisted gold torque, or neck ring, that looks for all the world like a length of rope (*page 136*); it is a symbol that goes back to the Bronze Age. Bludgeoning, hanging, strangling and drowning were also connected with rites at the bogs. The difference in method of death probably depended upon local custom and the particular ritual associated with the god or goddess being worshipped.

The goddess of fertility seems to have occupied an important place in the northern panoply deities right up until the first centuries after Christ. Then, apparently as a result of Celtic or Roman influences, her authority was challenged by that of an all-wise male deity: Wodan, or Odin, the god of death and battle, whose name survives in the word Wednesday.

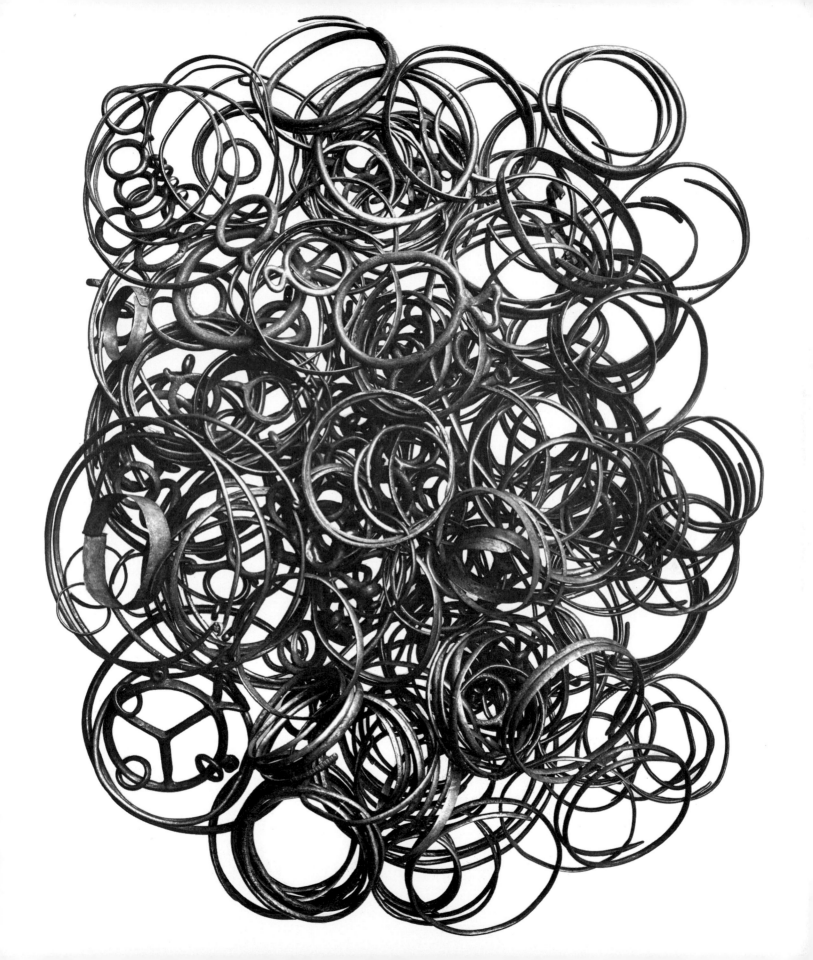

A Vehicle Fit for a Goddess
*Reassembled from pieces of two Iron Age wagons dug out of
a Jutland peat bog in the 1880s, this cart may have been
venerated by ancient Danes as a cult object—symbolizing the
vehicle used by the Mother Goddess on visits to earth.
Parts of similar wagons have since turned up in other bogs.*

Tacitus described the ritual surrounding the worship of Nerthus, or Mother Earth, by peoples living in Denmark. Her home was a sacred grove on an island in the sea, from which she was escorted at certain times of the year (though in just what form Tacitus did not make clear). She travelled in a chariot veiled with cloth that only a priest could touch. "The priest can feel the presence of the goddess in this holy of holies," Tacitus wrote, "and attends her with deepest reverence as her chariot is drawn along by cows. Then follow days of rejoicing and merrymaking in every place she condescends to visit. . . . No one goes to war, no one takes up arms; every iron object is locked away. Then, and then only, are peace and quiet known and welcomed, until the goddess, when she has had enough of the society of men, is restored to her sacred precinct by the priest." At this point, chariot, vestments, even the goddess herself ("Believe it if you will," noted the sceptical Tacitus) are cleansed in a secluded lake, and those charged with this sacred task are immediately drowned. "Thus," concluded Tacitus, "mystery begets terror

and a pious reluctance to ask what that sight can be which is seen only by men doomed to die."

Almost certainly the rôle of attendant was played by the most famous of all the bog people, the one known as Tollund man (*pages 152-153*). Discovered by peat cutters in Tollund Bog in central Jutland in 1950, the body was at first thought to be that of a recent murder victim. But a cautious police lieutenant had the wit to put in a call to Professor P. V. Glob, the man who had excavated the farming village at Barkaer. Since Professor Glob was lecturing at nearby Aarhus University at the time, he was able to come at once. He later described what he saw on his arrival at the bog—a desolate place surrounded by high, heather-clad hills:

"In the peat cut, nearly seven feet down, lay a human figure in a crouched position, still half buried. A foot and a shoulder protruded, perfectly preserved but dark brown in colour like the surrounding peat, which had dyed the skin. Carefully we removed more peat, and a bowed head came into view. As dusk fell, we saw in the fading light a man take shape before

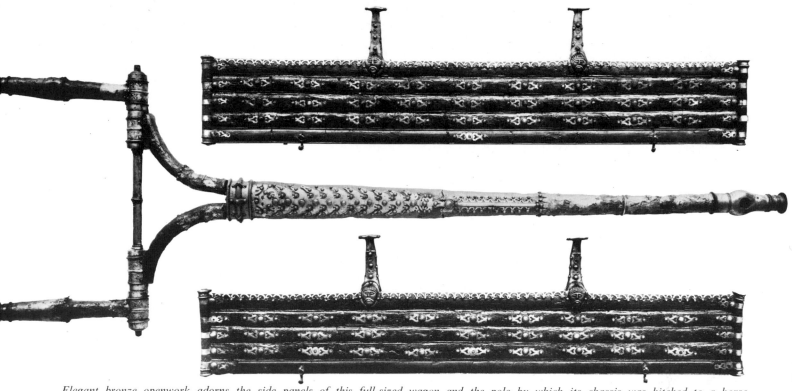

Elegant bronze openwork adorns the side panels of this full-sized wagon and the pole by which its chassis was hitched to a horse.

us. He was curled up, with legs drawn under him and arms bent, resting on his side as if asleep. His eyes were peacefully shut." But, Glob observed, "his brows were furrowed and his mouth showed a slightly irritated quirk, as if he were not overpleased by this unexpected disturbance of his rest".

Tollund man was naked except for a leather cap on his head, a leather belt around his waist and a braided leather rope around his neck—the rope with which he had been hanged or strangled.

Covered over again with peat to prevent the air from destroying it, the body was crated and taken to the Danish National Museum. There Tollund man was minutely studied. The prints of his fingers, the stubble on his chin and the furrows that creased his brow were all there to see. His face in fact was startling in its reality—not the portrait of a man but the man himself, all but ready to open his eyes and speak of the world he knew 2,000 years ago (*page 124*).

Because of his delicate features and fine hands, unmarked by heavy labour, Tollund man is thought to have been a village elder or priest. In ancient cultures, people of high rank were sometimes sacrificed in the belief that their special powers would benefit the community. From an autopsy performed on Tollund man, it appears that he was fed a special meal 12 to 24 hours before he died. The meal consisted of a gruel made of many different kinds of grain and seeds—some wild, some cultivated—"just those seeds", observed Professor Glob, "which were made to germinate, grow and ripen by the goddess's journey through the spring landscape". It is on evidence such as this that Tollund man is thought to have served as a consort to a goddess during the spring planting festivities. Having escorted her chariot and eaten the ritual meal, he then played out the last act of the drama and was sacrificed so that the land might bring forth new life.

At the time he died, in the first century before Christ, Scandinavia's long isolation was coming to an end. The Celtic tribes—assailed on one flank by Germanic tribes and on the other by the Romans —had finally been subjugated by the armies of Julius Caesar. After a 500-year hiatus, the Northmen were again in touch with the peoples of the Mediterranean. The contacts are evident in the Roman artifacts that began to enter Scandinavia: swords and sword belts; hoards of coins; priceless objects of art in bronze, silver and glass fashioned by Roman craftsmen. Some of these artifacts undoubtedly were booty collected by the Northmen in raids on the Roman garrison towns along the Rhine. Others may have been the trophies northern warriors earned as Roman mercenaries. And no doubt some of the finest objects were brought as gifts by Roman emissaries to the leaders of friendly Scandinavian tribes or villages.

Along with this influx of Roman goods came Roman ideas and ways of doing things. Northern craftsmen gradually incorporated Roman motifs and techniques into their metalwork, replacing their former Celtic models. The centuries-old practice of cremation began falling into disuse as the Northmen adopted Roman ideas about death. Once more graves were well furnished, and the dead were laid in wooden coffins, accompanied by food and drink.

Meanwhile, the Northmen were becoming of vital concern to the Roman Empire, which had expanded to share a common boundary with them. In the dispatches of field generals and the accounts of men like Caesar and Tacitus, the Northmen were identified for posterity. Initially it was the Cimbri and Teutons whose names appeared in these reports; later it was the Goths, Lombards, Vandals, Burgundians and Franks. And it is in these same ancient documents that the chronicle is carried forward into those centuries when Scandinavia's growing population, flooded coastlines and shortage of good farmland forced the Northmen to abandon their homes and to descend in wave after wave upon the Mediterranean world —thereby affecting the course of modern history.

Grisly Victims of Iron Age Religious Rites

In March of 1839, a country journal called *Light Reading for the Danish Public* took on a sombre subject in an article entitled "The Disinterred Corpse". It described a body discovered three years earlier, pinioned by stakes to the bottom of a Jutland peat bog. The journal reported that the body had belonged to a woman thought to have been a witch and that the stakes had been used by superstitious villagers to prevent her ghost from rising to haunt them.

The body was not the first to be uncovered by a workman's shovel, and by no means the last. Nearly 700 bog people have now come to light. Scientists have established that they are the remains of humans sacrificed as long as 2,400 years ago. Yet sceptics today still cling to quainter notions: that they are the bodies of Danes accused of being witches, murder victims or neighbours who were lost in the bogs. What the scientists say, they contend, is simply impossible.

In 1952, when a body turned up near Grauballe, Denmark, local farmers insisted that it was one Red Christian, a town drunk who vanished on a night in 1887; an old woman swore she knew his face. The scientists and the doubting community debated until carbon-14 tests fixed the corpse's age at about 1,600 years. A newspaper pronounced the matter settled under a whimsical headline: RED CHRISTIAN KNOCKED OUT BY ATOMS.

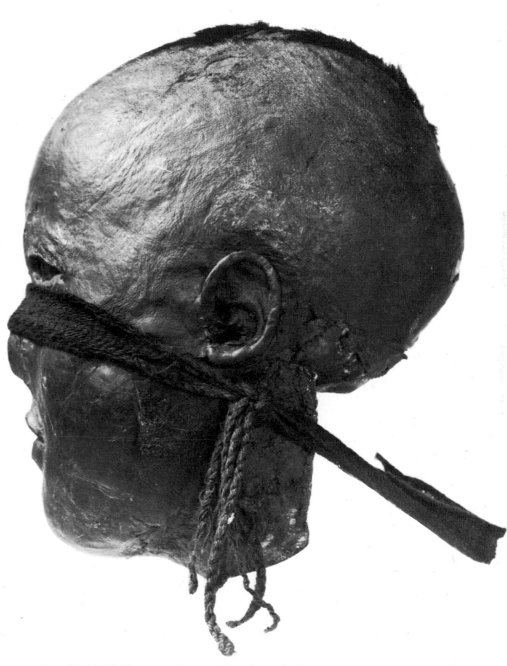

A woollen blindfold rests on the nose of a girl sacrificed in Schleswig-Holstein in the First Century A.D. *The girl's head was partly shaved before she was drowned (overleaf).*

The body of a young girl lies as she was found in 1952 at the bottom of a Schleswig-Holstein bog. Apparently she was placed in the bog alive and pinned down with birch branches and a large stone to drown her. Her face (profile on the preceding page) is almost entirely intact, as are her legs.

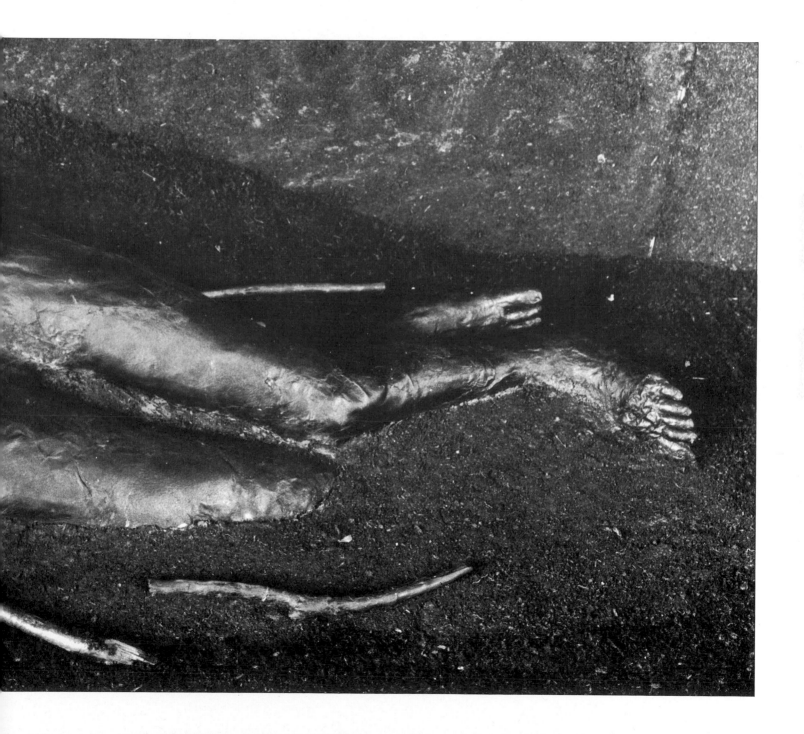

150

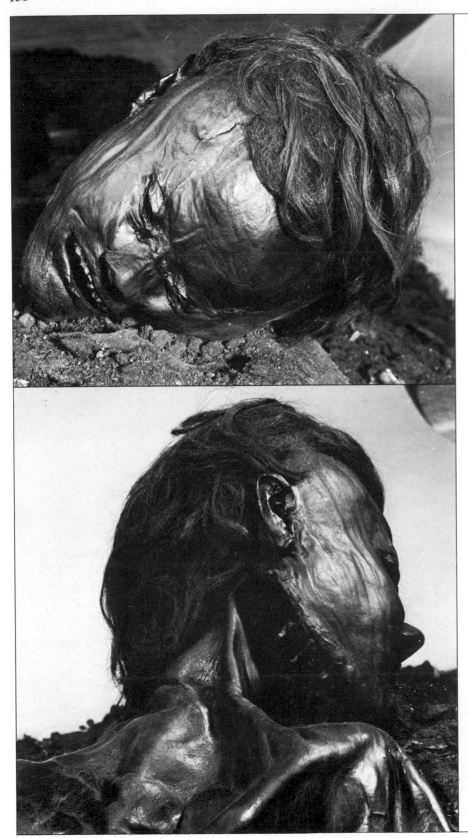

The head of the Grauballe man, so named for the village near which his body was uncovered in 1952, offers unmistakable evidence of a violent death: his throat had been slit almost from ear to ear (bottom left). Though the man met his end some 16 centuries ago, his agony—expressed by his furrowed brow and grimacing mouth (top left)—is still painfully vivid.

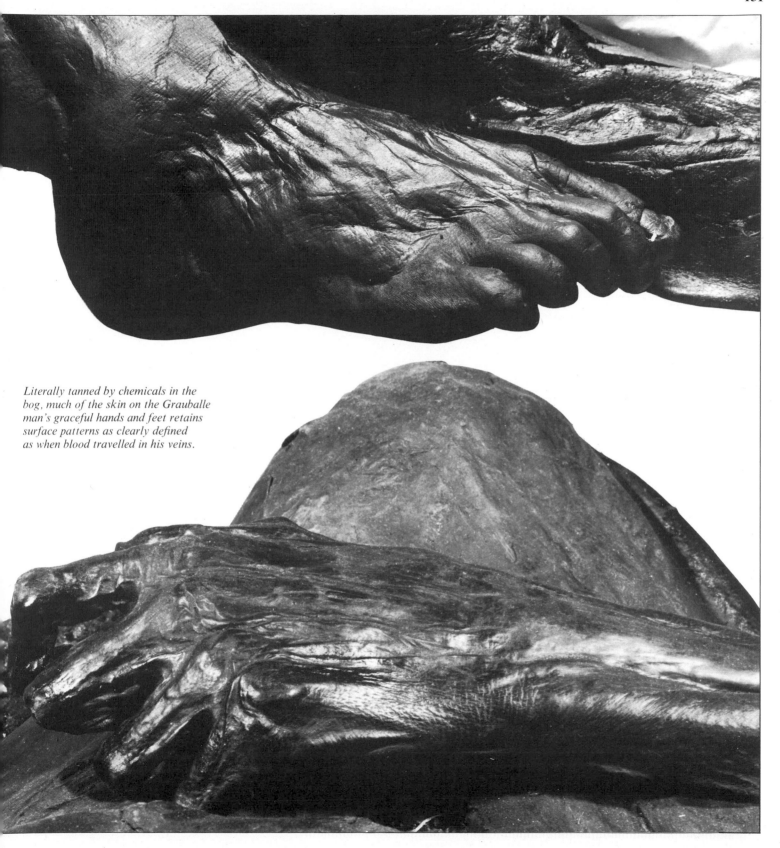

Literally tanned by chemicals in the bog, much of the skin on the Grauballe man's graceful hands and feet retains surface patterns as clearly defined as when blood travelled in his veins.

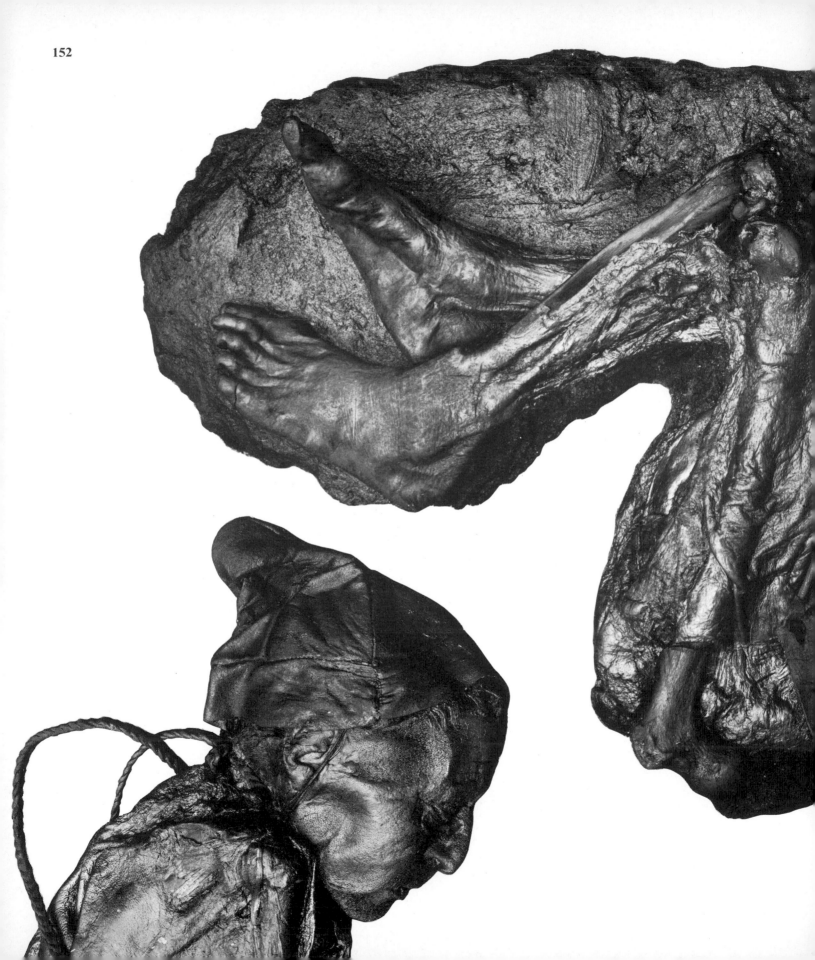

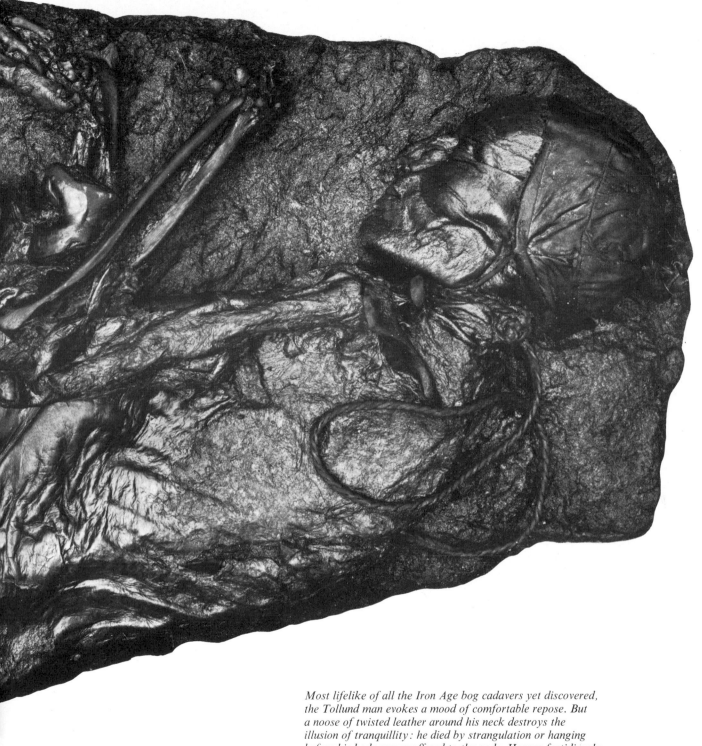

Most lifelike of all the Iron Age bog cadavers yet discovered, the Tollund man evokes a mood of comfortable repose. But a noose of twisted leather around his neck destroys the illusion of tranquillity: he died by strangulation or hanging before his body was proffered to the gods. He was fastidiously groomed for the sacrifice: hair cropped short, face shaved. When he was found in the bog, he was wearing only a loose hide belt at his waist and a stitched leather cap (left).

The Emergence of Man

This chart records the progression of life on earth from its first appearance in the warm waters of the new-formed planet through the evolution of man himself; it traces his physical, social, technological and intellectual development to the Christian era. To place these advances in commonly used chronological sequences, the column at the

Geology	Archaeology	Thousand Millions of Years Ago	
Precambrian earliest era		4.5	Creation of the Earth
		4	Formation of the primordial sea
			First life, single-celled algae and bacteria, appears in water
		3	
		2	
		1	
		Millions of Years Ago	
			First oxygen-breathing animals appear
		800	
			Primitive organisms develop interdependent specialized cells
Palaeozoic ancient life		600	Shell-bearing multicelled invertebrate animals appear
			Evolution of armoured fish, first animals to possess backbones
		400	Small amphibians venture on to land
			Reptiles and insects arise
			Thecodont, ancestor of dinosaurs, arises
Mesozoic middle life			Age of dinosaurs begins
		200	Birds appear
			Mammals live in shadow of dinosaurs
			Age of dinosaurs ends
		80	
Cainozoic recent life			Prosimians, earliest primates, develop in trees
		60	
		40	Monkeys and apes evolve
		20	
		10	Ramapithecus, oldest known primate with apparently man-like traits, evolves in India and Africa
		8	
		6	
		4	Australopithecus, closest primate ancestor to man, appears in Africa

Geology	Archaeology	Millions of Years Ago	
Lower Pleistocene oldest period of most recent epoch	**Lower Palaeolithic** oldest period of Old Stone Age	2	Oldest known tool fashioned by man in Africa
			First true man, Homo erectus, emerges in East Indies and Africa
		1	Homo erectus populates temperate zone
		Thousands of Years Ago	
Middle Pleistocene middle period of most recent epoch		800	Man learns to control and use fire
		600	
			Large-scale, organized elephant hunts staged in Europe
		400	Man begins to make artificial shelters from branches
		200	
Upper Pleistocene latest period of most recent epoch	**Middle Palaeolithic** middle period of Old Stone Age		Neanderthal man emerges in Europe
		80	
Last Ice Age		60	Ritual burials in Europe and Middle East suggest belief in afterlife
			Woolly mammoths hunted by Neandertha in northern Europe
		40	Cave bear becomes focus of cult in Euro
	Upper Palaeolithic latest period of Old Stone Age		Cro-Magnon man arises in Europe
			Asian hunters cross Bering Land Bridge to populate New World
			Oldest known written record, lunar notations on bone, made in Europe
			Man reaches Australia
			First artists decorate walls and ceilings of caves in France and Spain
		30	Figurines sculpted for nature worship
		20	Invention of needle makes sewing possible
			Bison hunting begins on Great Plains of North America
Holocene present epoch	**Mesolithic** Middle Stone Age	10	Bow and arrow invented in Europe
			Pottery first made in Japan

Four thousand million years ago

Three thousand million years ago

Origin of the Earth (4,500 million)

First life (3,500 million)

left of each of the chart's four sections identifies the great geological eras into which the earth's history is divided by scientists, while the second column lists the archaeological ages of human history. The key dates in the rise of life and of man's outstanding accomplishments appear in the third column (years and events mentioned in this volume of The Emergence of Man appear in bold type). The chart is not to scale; the reason is made clear by the bar below, which represents in linear scale the 4,500 million years spanned by the chart—on the scaled bar, the portion relating to the total period of known human existence (*far right*) is too small to be distinguished.

Geology	Archaeology	Years B.C.	
Holocene (cont.)	Neolithic New Stone Age	9000	
			Sheep domesticated in Middle East
			Dog domesticated in North America
		8000	Jericho, oldest known city, settled
			Goat domesticated in Persia
			Man cultivates his first crops, wheat and barley, in Middle East
		7000	Pattern of village life grows in Middle East
			Catal Hüyük, in what is now Turkey, becomes largest Neolithic city
			Loom invented in Middle East
			Cattle domesticated in Middle East
		6000	Agriculture begins to replace hunting in Europe
	Copper Age		Copper used in trade in Mediterranean area
			Corn cultivated in Mexico
		4800	Oldest known massive stone monument built in Brittany
		4000	Sail-propelled boats used in Egypt
			First city-states develop in Sumer
			Cylinder seals begin to be used as marks of identification in Middle East
		3500	First potatoes grown in South America
			Wheel originates in Sumer
			Man begins to cultivate rice in Far East
			Silk moth domesticated in China
			Horse domesticated in Central Asia
			Egyptian merchant trading ships start to ply the Mediterranean
			Pictograph writing invented in Middle East
	Bronze Age	3000	Bronze first used to make tools in Middle East
			City life spreads to Nile Valley
			Plough is developed in Middle East
			Accurate calendar based on stellar observation devised in Egypt
		2800	Stonehenge, most famous of ancient stone monuments, begun in England
			Pyramids built in Egypt
			Minoan navigators begin to venture into seas beyond the Mediterranean

Geology	Archaeology	Years B.C.	
Holocene (cont.)	Bronze Age (cont.)	2600	Variety of gods and heroes glorified in *Gilgamesh* and other epics in Middle East
		2500	Cities rise in the Indus Valley
			Earliest evidence of use of skis in Scandinavia
			Earliest written code of laws drawn up in Sumer
		2000	Use of bronze in Europe
			Chicken and elephant domesticated in Indus Valley
			Eskimo culture begins in Bering Strait area
		1500	Invention of ocean-going outrigger canoes enables man to reach islands of South Pacific
			Ceremonial bronze sculptures created in China
			Imperial government, ruling distant provinces, established by Hittites
		1400	Iron in use in Middle East
			First complete alphabet devised in script of the Ugarit people in Syria
			Hebrews introduce concept of monotheism
	Iron Age	1000	Reindeer domesticated in Eurasia
			Phoenicians spread alphabet
		900	
		800	Use of iron begins to spread throughout Europe
			First highway system built in Assyria
			Homer composes *Iliad* and *Odyssey*
			Mounted nomads appear in the Middle East as a new and powerful force
		700	Rome founded
			Wheel barrow invented in China
		200	Epics about India's gods and heroes, the *Mahabharata* and *Ramayana*, written
			Water wheel invented in Middle East
		0	Christian era begins

▼ Two thousand million years ago   ▼ One thousand million years ago

First oxygen-breathing animals (900 million) ▲   First animals to possess ▲ backbones (470 million)   First men (1.3 million) ▲

Credits

The sources for the illustrations in this book are shown below. Credits from left to right are separated by semicolons, from top to bottom by dashes.

Cover—Painting by Michael A. Hampshire, background photograph by Inga Aistrup. 8 —Erich Lessing from Magnum courtesy The Danish National Museum, Copenhagen. 12, 13—Paolo Koch from Rapho Guillumette. 15 —B. Primdahl. 16—Courtesy The Danish National Museum, Copenhagen. 19—Derek Bayes courtesy The British Museum, London. 20, 21—Maps prepared by Dr. S. A. Andersen, Geological Research Society, Copenhagen. 23 to 33—The Historical-Archaeological Research Centre at Roskilde. 34—Courtesy The Danish National Museum, Copenhagen. 38, 39—© Paal-Nils Nilsson/ TIOFOTO, Stockholm. 40—Courtesy The Danish National Museum, Copenhagen—Sören Hallgren for National Historical Museum/ ATA, Stockholm. 42—Tromsoe Museum, Tromsoe, Norway. 43—The Museum, University of Trondheim, Norway—University Museum of National Antiquities, University of Oslo. 45, 46—Courtesy The Danish National Museum, Copenhagen. 48 to 53—Paintings by Saul Lambert. 54—Lennart Larsen for The Danish National Museum, Copenhagen. 56 to 59—Courtesy The Danish National Museum, Copenhagen. 60 —Courtesy The Danish National Museum, Copenhagen, except centre, courtesy National Historical Museum, Stockholm. 62, 63 —Courtesy The Danish National Museum, Copenhagen, except top page 62, Lennart Larsen for The Danish National Museum, Copenhagen. 64—Inga Aistrup. 67—Courtesy The Danish National Museum, Copenhagen. 69, 70—© Paal-Nils Nilsson/TIOFOTO, Stockholm. 71—Courtesy Professor Bertil Almgren, Uppsala University. 72, 73—Courtesy The Danish National Museum, Copenhagen; © Paal-Nils Nilsson/TIOFOTO, Stockholm. 74 —Inga Aistrup. 76, 77—Courtesy National Historical Museum/ATA, Stockholm. 81 —Professor Maarten Stenberger. 82, 83 —Courtesy The Danish National Museum, Copenhagen. 85—Ken Kay courtesy Dr. Curt W. Beck, Vassar College. 86, 87—Ken Kay courtesy Dr. Curt W. Beck, Vassar College, except bottom left, Dr. Roman Vishniac. 88 —Erich Lessing from Magnum courtesy The Danish National Museum, Copenhagen. 89 —Staatsbibliothek, Berlin. 90, 91—Patrick Thurston courtesy The British Museum, London. 92—Erich Lessing from Magnum courtesy The Danish National Museum, Copenhagen. 94—Courtesy National Historical Museum/ATA, Stockholm. 96, 97—Erich Lessing from Magnum courtesy The Danish National Museum, Copenhagen. 99—Courtesy The Danish National Museum, Copenhagen. 100 —Erich Lessing from Magnum courtesy The Danish National Museum, Copenhagen. 101 —Erich Lessing from Magnum courtesy The Danish National Museum, Copenhagen; Courtesy The Danish National Museum, Copenhagen. 102—Erich Lessing from Magnum courtesy The Danish National Museum, Copenhagen. 105—Courtesy The Danish National Museum, Copenhagen—Courtesy National Historical Museum/ATA, Stockholm —Lennart Larsen for The Danish National Museum, Copenhagen. 106, 107—Erich Lessing from Magnum courtesy The Danish National Museum, Copenhagen. 108—Courtesy The Danish National Museum, Copenhagen. 109—Lennart Larsen for The Danish National Museum, Copenhagen—Courtesy The Danish National Museum, Copenhagen. 111, 112—Erich Lessing from Magnum courtesy The Danish National Museum, Copenhagen. 114—Courtesy The Danish National Museum, Copenhagen, drawing by Johannes Glob; Courtesy The Danish National Museum, Copenhagen. 115—Lennart Larsen for The Danish National Museum, Copenhagen. 117—Courtesy National Historical Museum, Stockholm. 119 to 123—Erich Lessing from Magnum courtesy The Danish National Museum, Copenhagen. 124—Courtesy The Danish National Museum, Copenhagen. 127 —Courtesy National Historical Museum/ ATA, Stockholm. 128, 129—Erich Lessing from Magnum courtesy The Danish National Museum, Copenhagen. 130—Courtesy The Danish National Museum, Copenhagen. 133 to 136—Erich Lessing from Magnum courtesy The Danish National Museum, Copenhagen. 138, 140, 143, 144, 145—Courtesy The Danish National Museum, Copenhagen. 147, 148, 149—Landesmuseum für Vor- und Frühgeschichte, Schloss Gottorf, Schleswig. 152, 153—Lennart Larsen for The Danish National Museum, Copenhagen.

Acknowledgments

For the help given in the preparation of this book, the editors are particularly indebted to Bertil Almgren, Head of the Department of North European Archaeology, Uppsala University, Uppsala, Sweden; Jens Bekmose, The Danish National Museum, Copenhagen; Arne Emil Christensen, First Assistant Keeper, Archaeological Department, University Museum of National Antiquities, University of Oslo; Ulf Erik Hagberg, Department of North European Archaeology, Uppsala University, Uppsala, Sweden; Poul Simonsen, Director of Tromsoe Museum, Tromsoe, Norway; C. Leif Vebaek, Curator of The Danish National Museum, Copenhagen. The editors also express their gratitude to The American Scandinavian Foundation, New York City; Mrs. Anna J. Andersen, widow of Dr. S. A. Andersen, The Danish Geological Research Society, Copenhagen; Curt W. Beck, Professor of Chemistry, Vassar College, Poughkeepsie, New York; Alessandro Bedini, Inspector, Superintendency of Antiquities, Rome; Gianfilippo Carettoni, Superintendent, Superintendency of Antiquities, Rome; Soeren Dyssegaard, Danish Information Office, New York City; P. V. Glob, Director, The Danish National Museum, Copenhagen; Hans Ole Hansen, Director of the Historical-Archaeological Research Centre at Roskilde, Denmark; Werner Hermann, Assistant, German Archaeological Institute; Sidney Horenstein, Scientific Assistant, The American Museum of Natural History, New York City; Ole Klindt-Jensen, Director, Prehistoric Museum, Moesgaard, Denmark; Ole Malling, Historical-Archaeological Research Centre at Roskilde, Denmark; Marinella Montagna-Pasquinucci, Institute of Prehistory, Pisa University, Pisa, Italy; Elisabet Munksgaard, Librarian, The Danish National Museum, Copenhagen; Svend Nielsen, The Danish National Museum, Copenhagen; Carin Orrling, National Historical Museum, Stockholm; Thorkild Ramskou, The Danish National Museum, Copenhagen; Brigitte Straubinger, the Antiquarian-Topographical Archives (ATA), Stockholm; Bernard Wailes, Associate Professor of Anthropology and Associate Curator of the University Museum, University of Pennsylvania, Philadelphia.

Bibliography

Bass, George F., ed., *A History of Seafaring*. Thames and Hudson, 1972.
Bibby, Geoffrey, *Four Thousand Years Ago*. Collins, 1962.
Brogger, A. W., and Shetelig, Haakon, *The Viking Ships: Their Ancestry and Evolution*. Translated from Norwegian by K. John, C. Hurst, 1972.
Butzer, Karl W., *Environment and Archaeology*. Methuen, 1972.
Caesar, Julius, *War Commentaries*. Ed. J. Warrington. Everyman's Library, 1965, Dent.
Carson, Rachel L., *The Sea Around Us*. Oxford University Press, 1961, Panther, 1969.
Childe, V. Gordon, *The Dawn of European Civilization*. Routledge, 1957.
Clark, Grahame, *The Stone Age Hunters*. Library of Early Civilizations. Thames and Hudson, 1967.
Coon, Carleton, S., *The Hunting Peoples*. Jonathan Cape, 1972.
Cornwall, Ian W., *Prehistoric Animals and*

Their Hunters. Faber, 1968.
Daniel, Glyn, *The Megalith Builders of Western Europe*. Kutchinson University Library, 1963. *Origins and Growth of Archaeology*. Penguin Books, 1967.
Davidson, Hilda Roderick Ellis, *Gods and Myths of Northern Europe*. Penguin Books, 1969.
Pagan Scandinavia. Thames and Hudson, (Ancient Peoples and Places), 1967.
Scandinavian Mythology. Paul Hamlyn, 1969.
Ehrich, R. W., ed., *Chronologies in Old World Archaeology*. University of Chicago Press, 1965.
Glob, P. V., *The Bog People; Iron Age Man Preserved*. Translated from the Danish by Rupert Bruce-Mitford, Faber, 1969.
Denmark: Danish Prehistoric Monuments:

Denmark from the Stone Age to the Vikings. Translated from the Danish by Joan Bulman, Faber, 1971.
Green, Roger Lancelyn, *Myths of the Norseman*. Bodley Head, 1962, Puffin and Penguin Books, 1970.
Hagen, Anders, *Norway*. (Ancient Peoples and Places). Thames and Hudson, 1967.
Kivikoski, Ella, *Finland*. Translated from the Finnish by Alan Binns, (Ancient Peoples and Places). Thames and Hudson, 1967.
Jensen, O. Klindt-, *Denmark before the Vikings*, (Ancient Peoples and Places). Thames and Hudson, 1957.
Landstrom, Bjorn, *The Ship*. Allen and Unwin, 1969.
Oxenstierna, Eric Graf, *The World of the*

Norsemen. Translated from the German by Janet Sondheimer. Weidenfeld and Nicolson, 1967.
Piggott, Stuart, *Ancient Europe*. Edinburgh University Press, 1965.
Polome, Edgar, C., ed., *Old Norse Literature and Mythology*. University of Texas Press, 1970.
Singer, Charles E., ed., *A History of Technology*. Oxford University Press, 1954.
Somme, A., *A Geography of Norden*. Heinemann Educational Books, 1969.
Tacitus, *The Agricola and the Germania*. Translated from the Latin by H. Mattingley, Penguin Books, 1970.
Wilson, David McKenzie, *The Vikings and Their Origins*. Thames and Hudson, 1970.

Index

Typesetting by C. E. Dawkins (Typesetters) Ltd., London SE1
Printed and bound in Belgium by Brepols Fabrieken N.V.